My Encounters With the Light

Jesus and the Janitor

My Encounters With the Light

Myles D. Ferguson

1999
Galde Press, Inc.
Lakeville, Minnesota

First Edition
First Printing, 1999

Library of Congress Cataloging-in-Publication Data
Ferguson, Myles D., 1939–
My encounters with the Light : Jesus and the janitor / Myles D. Ferguson.
p. cm.
ISBN 1–880090–36–8 (trade pbk.)
1. Ferguson, Myles D., 1939– . 2. Psychics—United States—Biography. 3. Parapsychology. 4. Occultism. I. Title.
BF1027.F47A3 1996
133.8'092—dc20 96–36183
CIP

Galde Press, Inc.
PO Box 460
Lakeville, Minnesota 55044-0460

Contents

Foreword

When Myles D. Ferguson asked me to edit his book, I said okay—as a favor to a friend. What a surprise! Although publishing is my business, nothing quite like Myles' book has ever come across my desk. I simply said, "Wow! This is a small book, but it's a *great book!*"

What's so great about it? Well, I once had a life-changing experience that resembles his meeting with Jesus. Whether or not I actually met Jesus on the astral plane (as Myles calls it), I'll never know. Principles, not individual personalities, seem to be the law of the spiritual domain which, I believe, is what separates it from the psychic level, which often deals with personalities.

My encounter with the radiant being with long hair and beard, who emanated pure white light and ensconced my self with love, took place on October 22, 1960, when I was twenty-five years old. I was a lost soul seeking direction, meaning, purpose and a goal in life. One morning in heartfelt agony I said aloud, "My God—if there is a God—please prove yourself to me!"

Instantly, I was splashed with cold water that seemed to come from nowhere in my apartment in Hollywood,

California. Later, around midnight, I lay on my bed, fully dressed with the lights on, and projected from my body to a plane on which a being who looked like Jesus and may have been Jesus greeted and welcomed me. He took me before a great light that reminded me of the sun—except it had no heat; rather, it was intelligent and seemed to vibrate messages (I interpreted my message in English).

In my psychic body I stood before this light and felt a ray of it enter my heart area, infusing my entire being with love and energy. I asked, "How can I repeat this experience?" Three years after I had returned to my body and normal life, I found and joined the Rosicrucian fraternity and studied the Way of the Rose and Cross.

Along the path to enlightenment, a path I am still pursuing, I had many experiences similar to those about which Myles writes in this book. Included were several UFO encounters, a few (although rare) glimpses of life in different historical eras, and even potential "past-life" incarnations that may or may not have been my own.

Like Myles, I also reached a point of empathy with the animal kingdom very early in life, and consequently have never understood or condoned the blood sport of hunting or war, which seem to feed from the same base nature deeply rooted in much of the human race.

My own feeling is that seeing Jesus was not what was so important. Having a change of heart was what was so important for such an encounter leaves one with two major goals, both difficult to achieve in this world:

Light of Reason: understanding both the physical and spiritual nature of All-Being.

Unconditional Love: practicing the old adage, "With Love, all things are possible."

I belong to no religion, yet have deep reverence for intelligence in all forms of expression. Yes, I concur with Myles that intelligence is as vast as the universe, even if men at this point use only about one-tenth of their mental capacities to explore, understand and master life intelligently.

While reading, later editing, the manuscript written by Myles, I was reminded of a Biblical saying familiar to most people in the Western world: "Behold, I stand at the door. Knock and it shall be opened. Ask and ye shall receive."

Jesus said those words.

To me, they mean symbolically that the neophyte who is filled with questions stands on a threshold, wondering who he really is, where he came from, and where he is going.

He becomes a walking question mark!

Instead of suppressing the questions, he begins to explore life in quest for the answers. That is what is meant by knocking on the door. The door is the human mind. Once the door is opened and mind becomes activated, the student begins to receive.

What does he or she receive? I like the line from the Rosicrucian chaplain's speech to exemplify my response: In the human consciousness were reflected the glories of the universe.

Myles shares some of the glories he has discovered, both through his encounters with Jesus and through daring to open his mind and become a walking question mark.

Once you've read these pages, you'll probably also become a walking question mark, traveling your own path to enlightenment, making your own individual discoveries.

This book inspires readers to lift their eyes toward the cosmic sun—and that's why it is a great book, even if it's small enough to slip into a pocket or purse.

WANDA SUE PARROTT

Springfield, Missouri
October 22, 1998

Chapter 1

The Jesus Encounters

When I was about forty-three years old, I was stumbling along on the spiritual path to enlightenment, which we all must do on our long journey back to the Creator. I was enduring the Dark Night of the Soul which marks the darkest time in a human being's life, after which time we emerge into the Golden Dawn, or happy time.

During this dark time, I had been hearing taunting voices, one of which kept repeating, "I know you not."

I knew that Jesus the Christ had made that statement during His time on Earth, so in my ignorance I assumed the voice to be His.

If one understands the positive and negative forces of the universe, then one would know that like attracts like and unlike repels like.

At 3:00 in the morning, as I sat on the bed, the voice kept repeating, "I know you not," over and over. The voice, being a negative force, aroused my anger, which is also negative. The voice fed upon, and attracted to itself, the negative energy—and the louder I cursed the voice, the louder the voice became.

It was a terrible situation!

I then saw a brilliant flash of light. From the light emerged a form which began to float toward me. As it approached me the features became clearer—the long hair flowing down over the shoulders and the beard. As Jesus the Christ came toward me, I lashed out at Him, shouting, "You say you know me not? Then I know you not!"

During this whole affair, his face radiated out love for me. He passed within inches of me and disappeared.

To this day I regret what I said, but now realize that Jesus appeared to me when I needed Him the most. As He said when he was here two thousand years ago: "Lo, I am with you even until the end of the earth."

And He *was* with me!

I am a member of the Association for Research and Enlightenment (A.R.E.) of Virginia Beach, Virginia. As a member, I received a free book that impressed me a great deal, *Witness To His Return* by G. Scott Sparrow. It is about personal encounters with Christ.

I was relieved to find many people, beside me, have had encounters similar to mine. At least I can relate my story without fear of being labeled a nut case.

One memorable story from *Witness To His Return* took place in 1940 and involved an eleven-year-old girl, Laura, whose parents were told their daughter was dying. Laura, her mother, and her brother had contracted scarlet fever; Laura's condition had progressed to spinal meningitis, for which no medical treatment was then available.

Doctors assured Laura's parents nothing could be done, and the child would die in terrible pain, screaming. The parents were advised not to be present during Laura's last days.

In the story, Laura remembers waving farewell to her parents and a Reverend Lang from her hospital bed and, after that, suffering with terrible pain. Later, after losing her eyesight, Laura lay on her right side. She heard a voice say from behind her, "Laura, turn over."

"No," she said. "It hurts too much to move. You come around to this side of the bed."

"I promise you it will not hurt," the voice replied. "Turn over!"

Laura obeyed and, turning, saw Jesus, whose hand reached out and touched her thin, twisted leg.

Later, Laura complimented a nurse about her pretty red hair. The nurse reacted with surprise that the girl had regained her sight and her health had improved. The nurse summoned doctors, who were dumfounded!

Laura recalls hearing the Reverend Lang tell his congregation about the dying little girl healed by Jesus. Today, as a sixty-two-year-old grandmother, Laura admits she had two more vivid encounters with Christ since her healing.

The following story, also from *Witness To His Return,* touched me deeply.

A woman identified only by her initials M.L.P. was lying in bed, praying, when she became distracted by a light in the hallway next to her bedroom. It seemed to be coming from down the hall and as it moved toward her bedroom its brightness increased.

Then she saw Jesus, who was carrying a candelabrum with seven lighted candles. She describes Jesus as tall and wearing a dark blue/purple robe with crescent moons and stars on it. The edge of the robe and its sleeves were trimmed with gold.

Jesus walked into M.L.P.'s room, placed His candelabrum on the floor, and knelt down in prayer by her bedside. She waved her right hand, touching His hair with a sensation she says she will always remember.

She remembers feeling engulfed with His love and the soft glow He and the candle radiated in the room.

He remained only a short time, then lifted the candelabrum and walked to the door.

M.L.P. asked, "How will I reach you again?"

Jesus turned, gave her a radiant smile, and said with eyes dancing, in a playful, loving tone of voice, "I'm in the phone book."

She watched Him walk away and wondered how He could be listed in the phone book, then realized He would be listed under the name "Emmanuel."

She looked in the dictionary and discovered the word Emmanuel meant "God is present in the world."

We know when reading the Bible that Jesus wept. We know He displayed anger when He overturned the money changers' tables in the church.

Now we know that Jesus has a sense of humor (after His encounter with M.L.P.).

Jesus is apparently well respected on the astral plane, and He is able to manifest physically on Earth at any time.

I once told two of my friends who are born again Christians about my Christ encounters. One of them told me I was going to hell and the other almost laughed me to scorn. I think the latter individual was angry and jealous because he had studied the Christian religion for many years and had never experienced a Christ encounter before.

I asked the former individual, "When is the next bus leaving for hell?"

As far as hell and a devil are concerned, these dogmatic religious situations do not exist except to those who believe they do.

For example: if one hundred million Americans believe in the devil and one hundred million do not believe, they who do believe will have created a devil which will have a form and consciousness.

Remember: We are co-creators with God.

The mass collective consciousness of those who believe in the Devil have created him. They will encounter him in their dreams, and some will encounter him in the waking state. They will encounter him because they created him.

However, those one hundred million Americans who do not believe will never encounter this devil!

Chapter 2

Laws of Karma and Reincarnation

I HAVE READ THE BIBLE six or seven times—from the start to the finish. It seems to me that God, in His infinite wisdom, never created a devil or an everlasting hell for His children who have erred.

However, God did set into motion certain immutable laws in the universe—and even though some of us do not believe in these laws, we are still governed by them.

The laws of karma (cause and effect) and reincarnation (energy is never lost, it only changes form) are two examples of these laws.

Therefore, many of the things that happen to us in a negative way are our own faults because of causes we ourselves initiated.

The Biblical "what you sow you will reap" and karma are the same law phrased in different language. And the word "reincarnation" (return to flesh) is a twentieth-century term that apparently was not used during the incarnation of the Master Jesus nearly two thousand years ago. According to Edgar Cayce, the word "resurrection" was the term used in the Bible to mean "many lifetimes."

There are many versions of the Bible today, including everything from the King James Version to modern-day easy language interpretations. Basically, in the Book of Matthew, the Disciples asked Jesus why the Jewish leaders insisted Elijah must return before the Messiah came. Jesus said they were correct, that the Messiah must come and set things in order. He also said Elijah had already come, but since he was not recognized he was badly treated by many people.

Jesus said he, the Messiah, would also suffer at their hands. The Disciples realized Jesus was referring to John the Baptist as the returned prophet Elijah.

The Book of John contains many mystical messages written in language that illustrated their principles in terms that the people of that time could appreciate. In John, the statement is made that only the Holy Spirit gives to man eternal life. It further says that those born only once, with physical birth, will never receive this gift.

John also contains passages in which Jesus was talking to his Disciples, telling them that in a short while He would be gone from the world, but he would still be present among them, for he would live again and so would they.

According to Edgar Cayce, popularly known as America's "Sleeping Prophet," Jesus himself lived approximately thirty lifetimes. His lives included, according to Cayce: Melchisedek, Joseph, Enoch, Jeshua, Joshua, and others, to name a few (from *Edgar Cayce's Story of Jesus* by Jeffrey Furst, 1968).

According to theories proposed by those who believe in the law of karma, some of the children who have been sexually molested in their present lifetimes were, themselves, the molesters in previous lives.

Recently there was a talk show on which discussions were held about child sexual molesters. Most of the people in the audience were under the impression that these offenders were homosexual.

Fortunately, there were a couple of experts in the audience who were knowledgeable about the subject; they informed everyone that ninety-five percent of such offenders are heterosexual. Mostly, they said, homosexual men were just interested in other men and the women in other women.

As I mention in this book, the concept of karmic law proposes that those who openly persecute homosexuals will find themselves being homosexuals in later lives, receiving the persecution they gave out.

Is it possible we will all be homosexual at one time or another in our long journeys back to the Creator? Besides living in many different countries and experiencing lifetimes as different races, will we also be living on other planets?

If so, by experiencing all these things we will attain a complete grasp of consciousness before returning to the Creator.

People sometimes ask me, "How can I return to the Creator in a hurry?"

My answer is, "Well, it takes aeons of time."

Religious Zealots and Karma

A good way to start is by helping others and being good to the people around you, always remembering: What we do to others, we are doing to ourselves.

I remember reading about a serial killer who killed almost one hundred people. It seems to me his would be the longer route back, but even he will eventually return to the Creator as we all will.

Some of the early explorers who came to the Americas brought their religion with them in their lust for gold. They attempted to force their religion down the throats of the native inhabitants in an "embrace or else" philosophy—meaning "kill them and take their gold."

Quite a religion, that was, with its followers violating its own tenets!

Such things have happened before—and are still going on today. For instance, around A.D. 1208, one of the world's most powerful religions was partly responsible for the massacre of about one million people who believed in karma and reincarnation. The Catholics and others were behind the killing of the Cathars.

When the army arrived in the city, the general asked a city official, "Which people should we kill?"

"Kill them all!" the man said. "God will sort them out."

The Cathars of Europe were industrious and owned large estates. Part of the motive of the people who sent the army was to confiscate their wealth.

When I told this story to Christians, one man said, "Our religion would never do that!"

I said, "Read the history books."

Fortunately, in today's religious climate here in America, a massacre of this nature cannot happen.

When Richard the Lionhearted led his army against the forces of Moslem leader Saladin during the Crusades, he captured three thousand prisoners of war.

Richard then gave the order for them all to be put to the sword and slaughtered like so many cattle.

There was an outcry from the people of the known world as to why this was done.

This was an example of one horrendous deed someone performed because of his religious zeal.

I am sure that when you turn on your own television set in these modern times you see news that makes you aware that massacres of the same nature are occurring in today's world.

Many modern-day evangelists are lining their pockets with their followers' money in the name of Jesus—and going to jail for fraud.

They tell their followers to follow the dictates of their church and pour in the money or go to hell—a hell I do not believe exists.

I met a woman who, in her will, was leaving her house to an evangelist who was in jail. I thought to myself, "This is the height of ignorance. Better give her estate to the poor."

Questions about AIDS

I have heard stories about some followers of such evangelists and religions who are going into hospitals to visit AIDS victims. They tell the patients, "You are dying by virtue of the fact that you are homosexual."

Shame on these so-called religious people.

They make the victims feel guilty and tell them they are going to an eternal hell that doesn't even exist.

They tell the AIDS victims to renounce their homosexuality.

That would be the same thing as asking me to renounce my heterosexuality, which I would not do—and could not do—any more than homosexuals would or could renounce their sexual preference.

Actually, many heterosexual people are becoming infected with the HIV virus that causes AIDS, with teenagers heading the list as the fastest-rising percentage of victims, along with elders who are infected through blood transfusions.

Many teenagers think they are invincible, so they do not use protection during sexual activity.

In New York City the number-one killer of women is not heart disease or cancer.

It is AIDS.

A girlfriend of mine who works at a hospital related one of the worst cases about AIDS:

"A couple married seven years ago," she said. "In the first year of marriage, the husband went out and had sex with another woman and became infected; then his wife also became infected, with neither knowing so."

For the next seven years they had a child for each of those seven years.

Now, all nine family members are dying from AIDS.

Recently, doctors were attempting to understand how a mother infected her two sons, ages nine and ten, with the HIV virus. When they were born, she was not infected.

Possibly, HIV is more easily spread than anyone thought.

Oral sex was once believed to be safe, but according to doctors who tested HIV on monkeys, the animals spread it to each other orally.

After telling the story of the HIV-spreading monkeys to some of my male friends, I could see their jaws dropping in disappointment. They thought oral sex was the last bastion of safety.

They would say, "Why can't a man have any fun any more with a God-given blessing?"

Maybe this is nature's way of saying, "You are killing off my animals and polluting my air and water, so now I'm going to get rid of some of you." Or, most of you.

There are entire communities in Africa where the only people left alive are the very young and the elderly, with the people between those groups all dead or dying from AIDS.

Whether AIDS ever gets that bad in America remains to be seen.

The good news seems to be that, as of October 1998, the explosive AIDS epidemic appears to be on the decline or at least in check because of drugs that effectively slow its progress.

Is An Ounce of Prevention Worth a Pound of Cure?

Another disease on the increase, which my mother has, is chronic fatigue syndrome (CFS).

I have heard that Edgar Cayce gave a reading on CFS, stating that it is caused by a lack of magnesium, and the best way to deal with it is to take magnesium, the full range of amino acids and beet broth.

For most of her life, my mother did not take vitamin or mineral supplements, and that is probably where the problem lies. The soil where the crops are grown in California and elsewhere are vastly depleted of minerals because of decades of over-planting.

More than one hundred diseases have been identified as being caused by a vitamin or mineral deficiency. For that reason, I strongly recommend everyone consider taking supplements.

Recent statistics stated that the average doctor lives about fifty-five or sixty years, while the average man in the neighborhood lives about seventy-five years.

Many doctors will tell us that as long as we eat balanced meals there is no need to take vitamins.

It appears to me that they are dead wrong!

If everyone took supplements, many doctors would be out of work. They would no longer be able to make their mortgage payments on their estates or drive their Mercedes Benz cars.

A doctor spends about eight years going to medical school and taking out loans while attending.

Someone once asked me, "How long would it take a doctor to repay his loans once he goes to work?

I replied, "About a week!"

(Of course, that is an exaggeration…isn't it?)

How Edgar Cayce Worked

As I mentioned previously, I have been a member of the Association for Research and Enlightenment for many years. This organization is built around the life and good works of Edgar Cayce, who gave about fourteen thousand readings during his lifetime.

After attending many Edgar Cayce study groups, I heard that if a person was sick and the doctors could not help him or her, the team of attending physicians might write to Edgar, asking for his help. Private individuals who could not be helped by doctors frequently wrote, asking for help.

Both the patients and doctors seeking Cayce's diagnoses were usually unknown strangers who had heard about Edgar's gift.

Cayce would give a reading by lying down on his back while his wife Gertrude sat down with the letter, and pad and pencil nearby.

Edgar would go into a trance.

Gertrude would read the letter, explaining the problem; she would then give the patient's address.

Edgar would travel out of his physical body to the address given and enter into the body of the patient, where he would locate the problem, diagnose the condition, and recommend a procedure for the patient to follow to recover.

Edgar would then awaken, but did not remember anything he said during the trance.

Gertrude Cayce, however, wrote down everything Edgar had said during the trance/diagnosis.

Edgar Cayce was about ninety-eight percent correct in his diagnoses of patients' illnesses, while doctors were only about fifty percent correct in theirs.

The fact that Edgar had no schooling in the medical field, while doctors had to spend eight years of study, made many of them dislike him.

They labeled Edgar Cayce "the freak."

I heard that in one case a child was having terrible pains in her stomach and four of the top surgeons had recommended immediate surgery.

The parents of the child went to get a reading from Cayce, who said the condition would clear up if a glass of water with half a lemon were taken daily.

When the surgeons learned what Cayce had said, they told the newspapers to print it, in an effort to make Edgar look like a fool.

The girl, who followed Cayce's advice, recovered a week later.

Cayce was warned in a reading not to give more than one or two readings per day because of the powerful forces involved, but because he loved his fellow man and wanted to help people, he gave many more than that.

When Edgar Cayce died in 1945 and passed over to the other side, was a long rest required because he had pushed himself beyond the limits that were recommended?

Edgar Cayce's life of service had begun when he was a young man and had read the Bible many times from cover to cover.

One day, while sitting alone in a wooded area, an angel appeared to him, telling Edgar that God was pleased with him and wished to grant him one wish.

Most men would have said "wealth" for their wish, but Cayce only wanted "to help my fellow man."

That one wish was granted.

Karmic Cause and Effect As Natural Law

Was Edgar Cayce's premature demise—like many other illnesses and diseases people experience—a demonstration of karmic law in its operation as "cause and effect" in motion?

If so, by relieving stress, or changing one's dietary or other unhealthful habits, can conditions that could lead to disease and death be reversed? If the cause of a problem is eradicated, can ill effects be reversed? How is your karma related to your health?

Karma Is Everywhere

Karma affects us all, often in ways that don't seem karmic at all!

In the early 1960s I went through a bad divorce involving two years of court battles with my three lawyers and my ex-wife's two attorneys.

When it was over, I filed bankruptcy against all the lawyers who were eating me alive and all the credit card charges that we both stacked up.

Later, someone asked me what was the difference between a dead dog and a lawyer.

"I don't know the answer," I said. "What is the difference between a dead dog and a dead lawyer?"

He said, "There are skid marks in front of a dead dog."

Of course, that is his opinion, not necessarily mine.

When we cheat others, even if it is done legally—as in my case—then we will have to meet ourselves later.

Karma!

It's a natural law we can recognize at work in our lives when we are aware of the principle of cause and effect, as happened in my case.

A number of years after my divorce and bankruptcy filing, I had completely restored an old Cadillac which was parked on Burbank Boulevard in Burbank, California.

One morning the police came knocking on my door at 3:00 A.M. to inform me that a drunk driver had hit my car from behind, and the entire rear end of my Cadillac was sitting on the ground.

The driver of a large station wagon had backed away from the wreck and driven to the house of a friend. The police followed the trail of water from the station wagon's broken radiator and arrested him. The driver was from south of the border. He had no insurance or driver's license. The Cadillac represented a major investment and I lost a large amount of money.

I feel the bankruptcy I filed to avoid paying attorney's fees and credit card charges (which I owed) was the cause, and the loss of my car was the effect of karma, since the amounts I owed and lost were just about the same (equal) amounts!

Justice—Another Name for Karmic Law?

I saw on the news the story in which Lorena Bobbit cut off her husband's penis here in the United States during the early 1990s.

It is difficult for me to understand how a woman could resort to such an action. Maybe it was from hatred of the man for his infidelity or other abuse, but the story did not stop in the U.S. with that one incident.

When news of the Bobbit incident was televised on international television, it was shown on a station in Bangkok, Thailand, inspiring one hundred women from Thailand to commit copycat acts by also cutting off their husbands' penises.

I've read reports about Thai men (and men in other countries) being the king of the roost and women are looked down upon—much more so than here in America.

Were these women who imitated Lorena Bobbit's act taking justice into their own hands?

These women probably were badly abused, but if the law of karmic justice applies in their cases, what might happen?

As I understand karma, as explained by Edgar Cayce, we should be careful about what we hate because we are certain to become it. If we inflict harm, we may be likewise harmed.

By this reasoning, in later lifetimes when these women are men, they may have to undergo the same ordeals they caused their men.

Bangkok, for years, has been called "The Sex Capital of the World," with men from all over the globe going there for that reason.

I have talked with several men who travel all over the world to many countries. Their consensus is that Bangkok and Southern California have the most beautiful women in the world.

It is probable that more than half the prostitutes in Bangkok are infested with the HIV virus that causes AIDS.

Of course, there are prostitutes in most countries, prostitution being known as the "world's oldest profession."

I heard a report on the radio that more than half the prostitutes in America are also infected with the HIV virus.

So, let's look at the sexual side of karma on a global scale.

Global Karma and Sex

Japanese men are notorious for not wearing condoms, probably because they simply do not enjoy wearing them. This, of course, puts them at higher risk for contracting sexually transmitted disease.

When I was in Waikiki, Hawaii, about seventy percent of the tourists I saw on the beach were Japanese, and many of them travel to Bangkok.

In some parts of Thailand there are families in deep poverty, and when a daughter is born she is destined to be sold later into a prostitution ring for a hefty sum of money, probably more than her father can earn in a number of years of labor.

Many of the working men of Thailand have visited the brothels and contracted HIV, passing it on to their wives.

This is not exclusive to Thailand.

It is happening to many people in all parts of the world.

Most people, wherever they may be, are good, and that includes Thailand, which is an industrious society.

Once when I was returning by shuttle from the airport, a gentleman sitting next to me said, "My wife threatened to cut off my penis if she ever catches me cheating on her."

"If I had a girlfriend or wife who threatened me in the same way, I would leave her for good before the sun ever went down," I said. "I plan to keep mine until it is time to check out from planet Earth!"

Treating the opposite sex with kindness and respect makes good sense—and good karma.

Karma in History

For several hundred years after Jesus left the Earth, many of the world's religions taught to the masses the doctrines of karma and resurrection (reincarnation). It is, however, a known historical fact that in A.D. 553 the church fathers of the world met at Constantinople and removed the doctrines of karma and resurrection because they were becoming increasingly embarrassing to their church teachings.

It is a fact also that today the majority of the world's population believes in the law of reincarnation!

I have attended several different Edgar Cayce Search for God study meetings held in various private homes and rented conference rooms.

Many events pertaining to Edgar Cayce were discussed including his predictions, the breakup of Atlantis and Lemuria, his thousands of readings about health, past lives, karma, etc.

I heard that we are not allowed to remember our past lives because if we remembered some of the things we did to others, the guilt we could feel could affect us in a terrible way.

We are never burdened with more negative karma than we can handle, and most of us have many more blessings than misfortunes.

One of the interesting things about reincarnation is the homosexual situation as it exists today in the world. I have heard that we may choose to live several lifetimes as a woman and then to switch over to living several as a man to help gain a full grasp of life's many experiences.

After we have switched over from living several lifetimes of a woman, during the first life as a man we have a strong desire for a man because we have been with men for so long. Usually in the second lifetime as a man we begin to desire a woman. This is one cause of homosexuality.

We should never judge others by their sexual preference. Some of the world's greatest people were homosexual.

Another cause of this condition is where an individual has openly persecuted homosexuals in one lifetime and in a later incarnation finds himself in a similar position receiving the persecution he gave out, a case of our karma being balanced.

I have heard that during Roman times there were groups of Romans who would go to other areas and countries where they would capture people and animals for the Roman arenas.

Once in the arenas men would fight other men and animals to the death. People who capture others and place them in captivity will themselves be placed in captivity at a later time or lifetime, to balance the karma.

Many of the Romans would sit in the arenas and watch the lions tear men apart and would get a perverse enjoyment out of the spectacle. These Romans paid for their enjoyment in later lifetimes by experiencing physical ailments.

One time I rented a video on champion kick boxing and I saw men badly injured in these real-life contests. I also realized that some people enjoy watching these men get hurt as the Romans did, but I never again watched this sort of thing because I found it very appalling.

During the time of the arenas, the Romans were reaching new heights of debauchery. In recorded history eighteen out of twenty-one civilizations collapsed from within, and the Romans were approaching that end.

The Roman military was comprised of mostly mercenary soldiers with some voluntary Roman citizens.

Today in America, our citizens volunteer to enter the military instead of being drafted, which is a better idea for those who do not wish to kill others or be killed.

I heard that during the Crusades many people were bored with life so they volunteered to join the crusading armies to experience some adventure in their lives.

But instead they experienced the horrors of war. Because they volunteered instead of being conscripted, they in effect volunteered to kill other human beings and in later lifetimes they had to meet some unpleasant karma in other wars.

Everyone should use the law of moderation in all things.

I have heard that a person who has been a glutton in one experience will balance his karma by choosing to starve to death in a later experience.

I have heard that if a person is wealthy in one life but fails to help people less fortunate than himself, then in his next lifetime he will be in poverty.

Everyone should work at some kind of job or labor that is uplifting to their fellow human beings.

Some people fail to work because they are wealthy or they just do not like to work. I heard that these people will balance their karma by begging on the street in a later lifetime.

Factory owners who pay low wages to their employees should raise their wages or help their employees' families—or possibly find themselves in poverty in later lifetimes.

Some people who read these statements of karma and reincarnation will not accept them because their religions say there is no such thing.

Believe me, even if people do not accept it, their lives are still governed by the laws of karma and reincarnation and we will live again.

Chapter 3

The Essenes

In 1947 the Dead Sea Scrolls were discovered. World scholars went to work in an effort to decipher the scrolls. Recently there was information shown on television about this work. The information given by the scholars, and by author Jeffrey Furst, was that Jesus the Christ and his mother Mary were both members of the Essene community, forty miles outside of Jerusalem, in Qumran.

The Essenes wrote the Dead Sea Scrolls.

According to Jeffrey Furst in *Edgar Cayce's Story of Jesus,* the Essenes were the highest evolved organization on the planet at that time, which is why Jesus chose to be born into the fold of the Essenes.

During the Crucifixion, Emperor Tiberius of Rome sent a last-minute reprieve ordering Jesus to be taken down from the cross because of lack of evidence against him. This theory has recently circulated, but it was not repeated by the above-quoted Jeffrey Furst. It claims that some of the followers of Jesus, and members of esoteric secret spiritual organizations, were there to take Him to a secret hiding place, because there were those who still wanted Jesus dead.

After recovering His health, Jesus allegedly raised a family and later died of old age.

When Jesus was baptized by John the Baptist, He received the Holy Ghost and had the ability to perform miracles.

During the Crucifixion the Holy Ghost re-ascended.

Between these two events He was Jesus the Christ.

Before and after these two events, he was Jesus the man.

To give an analogy: When Thomas Jefferson was not the president, he was Thomas Jefferson the man, but when he became President of the United States, he was Thomas Jefferson the president.

It will be a hard pill to swallow for some religions that claim Jesus died on the cross for their sins when, in fact, he didn't die at all on the cross, and each and every one of us is personally responsible for our own errors.

Our errors will be forgiven but not forgotten, because we are governed by the law of karma and many lifetimes are sometimes required to balance the karma before we return to the Creator.

I have heard that people in many parts of Europe and the East believe that the Master Jesus is buried in a tomb in Kashmir and the Mother Mary is buried in Pakistan.

Thousands of people have visited these tombs.

As of 1998, several scholarly books were in wide circulation which allude to the possible secret burial site of Jesus as being in the Languedoc region of France. There, authors claim, he and his wife, best-known as the Biblical Mary Magdalene, raised a family whose descendants may or may not someday be proven as historically related to the Merovingian dynasty.

At the present time some of the most powerful religions in the world don't want their followers to find out that Jesus and Mary were Essenes and that Jesus did not die on the cross. They want this information suppressed and they are spending vast sums of money to do so.

Otherwise they might lose control of their followers who would find out that they have been preaching false doctrines for hundreds and hundreds of years.

Anyone familiar with history would know that, after the Romans sacked Jerusalem, they took a contingent of troops and attacked the inhabitants of the Essene community at Qumran.

Chapter 4

My Spiritual Quest

Before we are born again on the earth plane, we choose our parents and they choose us on an unconscious level.

This is done so that we can find a suitable environment in which to work within for our karma. We usually reincarnate in large groups with our friends as well as enemies (from previous lifetimes) because we are supposed to learn to get along with everyone.

In a previous lifetime I punched one of my children, so at the age of fifteen in this lifetime my father punched me in the face.

What I had sowed, I reaped.

However, now that I am six feet two inches tall and weigh 220 pounds, and he is five feet eight inches and

160 pounds, you can see why my father never attempted it again!

During the first two years of life, our consciousness travels back and forth between our baby body and the astral planes.

The reason for this is that we were in the astral planes for a time, carrying on with certain activities that we are now concluding.

After the second year of life, we begin to settle down and prepare for the life ahead.

I remember being a kindergarten student in Washington Grammar School, Burbank, California. I punched a student who was much bigger than me. I felt very powerful after that, but a few months later the same thing happened to me.

None of us can escape the immutable law of cause and effect.

When we use physical violence to solve our problems, then we will encounter more violence until we learn not to use it.

At the age of about six years, while living in Burbank, California, I lay down to take a nap, During this nap I experienced my first out-of-body experience (OBE) that I can recall. I was catapulted up into white fluffy clouds on a beautiful sunny day.

Every one of us leaves our bodies during sleep at night or during naps; however, most of us do not recall the event.

In most cases, only about twenty-five percent of the OBE event is fed back to the conscious mind of those who do recall such experiences.

At the age of seven I was living in West Covina, California, with my parents. One morning around 3:00 A.M. I awoke to see a figure standing next to my bed, at which time I sat up to observe it.

I could clearly see the outline of the head, shoulders and upper torso, but there were no features to the face. I was a little uneasy, so I lay back down and put the covers over my head.

As I sat back up to observe it again, the figure just seemed to fade away.

When we are in our younger years, we have these strange encounters because we are more open to them. When we tell our parents about it, they usually laugh at us or tell us these encounters just do not take place, so we begin to block them out of our consciousness.

By the age of twenty or so, most of us have completely blocked out the possibility of any strange encounters.

In order to reawaken our psychic abilities, we must learn to pray, meditate and possibly associate ourselves with an esoteric mystery school where we may learn about the mysteries of the universe.

Prayer and Meditation

When we learn to pray and meditate, we are enriching the

lives of others and, therefore, enriching and bringing more peace into our own lives.

When groups or individuals pray in a given area of a city, the crime rate decreases in that area, with the police departments sometimes taking credit, according to news reports.

If the police were told about the meditation, would they believe that it has any positive effects?

Hideous Sights and Higher Planes

Many people have seen decaying human bodies that some consider to be hideous in appearance.

At death, the soul, which animates the body, pulls out and travels back to the higher planes in most cases.

The body, left behind, begins to decay with the atoms flying out in all directions.

The soul is clothed in the substance of the physical plane while it is here.

Virtually everyone leaves their bodies during sleep, with some going to the higher planes where they sometimes see grotesque bodies floating around.

As on the Earth, these are the bodies left behind by the souls who have gone on to a higher plane and no longer have need of a body.

As I mentioned, we are clothed in the substance of the plane in which we reside, and we should be aware that there are many planes of existence.

Many Planes

When she was just turning twenty, my friend Wanda Sue Parrott discovered the fact that there are many planes of existence and consciousness which humans can experience during an out-of-body projection.

The realization changed her life.

"When I tried to tell people I'd risen up and seen my body on the bed, they treated me like I was mentally unbalanced," she told me, "so for a long time, I didn't mention what had happened."

Most people don't discuss the OBE experience unless or until they meet others who are interested or also have had such conscious awareness of the phenomenon once called astral flight or astral projection.

Many people write their experiences in journals rather than talk about them.

I have tried to recount my experiences with the light—and other planes—in this book.

Fun and Friendship on the Astral Plane

In one of my OBE experiences I was flying about forty feet above the cars traveling north on the Golden State Freeway (Interstate 5) from Los Angeles to Northern California.

There was a man on my left and another on my right, both of whom were possibly also experiencing out-of-body travel. We were laughing and observing the different kinds of cars that were moving under us.

At other times I have flown over white sandy beaches, observing the sunbathers below.

I was going about thirty-five miles per hour and observing the scene from roughly sixty feet above the ground.

If you've ever dreamed you were flying, or soaring, face down above the sand, or going up and down a flight of stairs, perhaps you were having a similar experience.

Most people dream of flying.

Perhaps they really were!

One time I lay down on my back on the couch, around 5:30 P.M., for a quick nap. I left my body and was walking down the long hallway toward the other end.

Ahead of me appeared to be a black cloud that was approaching me. I fell backward. As soon as I impacted the floor, I was back in my body looking at the ceiling.

A full minute must have passed before I was able to move. It seemed I was experiencing a temporary form of physical paralysis.

Wanda Sue Parrot has also sensed such seeming paralysis after a projection experience. She explains it as the reintegration of the two polarities of self, the physical and counterpart non-physical aspects of the whole.

At another time in the late afternoon, I observed my curtains flowing back and forth. Someone was calling my name while I was in the borderline state on the same couch mentioned above.

A prominent psychologist from a California state mental institution told Wanda Sue, "Everyone hears voices."

According to his theory, the nature of the messages reflects whether the experience is normal and healthful or abnormal and psychotic.

Time, Space, and Mind

One morning when I came home from work around 9:30 A.M., I stretched out to take a nap. While in the borderline state I heard a voice say, "What do you dig, man?"

I immediately came back to the normal state of objective consciousness, thinking, "How interesting!"

I then went back into the borderline state and saw two girls and two guys sitting on the bed with me.

We talked among ourselves.

I had gone from being alone on the bed, coming out of the borderline state, slipping back into it, and engaging in the conversation in a few brief seconds.

This raises an issue with which scientists and mystics frequently deal, asking the question: What is the true nature of time, space and mind?

Wanda Sue, a very good fellow writer who was master of our Rosicrucian Lodge in San Fernando Valley in 1984 and 1985, moved to Missouri to care for aging relatives in 1988.

A few years after she moved, Wanda Sue had a remarkable OBE that seemed like a dream. She keeps a dream journal, and had written the following entry:

Sunday Morning

"I was on a sandy tropical beach with Myles Ferguson. It was night and a full moon was shining. It was a balmy, warm place I recognized instantly, even though I have never been there in person. It was Guadalcanal, and the beach where we were was horseshoe shaped, with tropical palm trees and other vegetation surrounding the sand, which seemed very white under the light of the full moon. Myles just suddenly appeared and, together, we gazed out toward the sea and were engulfed by energy of soothing, harmonizing perfect peace."

My friend copied her impression into a letter that she went right out and mailed that Sunday following the early-morning experience.

What she didn't know was that I too had experienced the same projection. I decided to call her that Sunday evening.

"I saw you in the borderline state," I said. "You were on a beach surrounded by palm trees."

"Myles, I had the same experience!" Wanda Sue said. "I sent you a letter about it. Do you know where you were?"

"Guadalcanal," I said.

"I was there, too. Read my letter. I wrote the name in the letter."

We decided that possibly we had projected there to gather energy.

Otherwise, why would two friends who live nearly 1,600 miles apart take a moonlight vacation, free of charge, on a sandy beach that had been controlled by the Japanese military during World War II?

Obviously time, space and mind played a role in the mutual projection—all limitations vanished!

If we had been sweethearts, we might have considered the meeting romantic in nature, but Wanda Sue and I are platonic friends who aren't interested in sneaking kisses on a moonlit tropical isle—at least not with each other!

Stretching the Truth

At another time, Wanda Sue and I wondered just how far we could actually stretch truth. It happened in California in 1985, after we had left the Sunday night meeting at our lodge and were talking in the parking lot long after most others had left.

When Wanda Sue started to unlock the door of her Honda Civic, she realized that the key was locked inside the vehicle. The only open window was a small wind wing in the rear of the vehicle, not large enough for a person to get in, and too far from the ignition for an arm to reach.

Rosicrucians perform lots of experiments and that's what Wanda Sue decided to do."If I stand stiff like a board, Myles, but allow all the cells in my body to be like plastic, will you try to push me through the small slot, feet first?"

She was joking, trying to lighten the moment because we both knew we'd have to call the Auto Club to rescue her—which meant a long wait in a dark parking lot.

"Okay," I said.

Things happened so fast that neither of us recalls the specific details. Suddenly Wanda Sue's head was inside the car and I was pushing her by the feet so her body moved forward over the back of the driver's seat.

Her body seemed to grow longer and thinner, but once she was into the front seat she began to coil up like a snake.

Suddenly she called,"I've got the keys!"

She opened the door from the driver's inside handle and pulled herself out of the car. We were facing each other, eye to eye, and laughing as she dangled the keys before me.

Then Wanda Sue shrank a full foot! She went from around six feet five inches to her normal five feet six inches.

She got back in, sitting in the ordinary driver's position, and started the car. We waved good night and went our separate ways—just as if nothing extraordinary had happened.

Ten years later we were still wondering, however, if we could perform such a demonstration if we had an audience.

Or, does truth stretch only when a need exists?

Looking at Levitation

Wanda Sue told me she had asked questions about the nature of matter ever since, as a child of around eight or nine, she witnessed a heavy wood dining room table elevate from the floor and glide across a room, settling in the corner.

She, her ten-year-old friend Carol Hasley, and four elderly women who had been holding a seance in which they asked "yes" and "no" questions had to push and tug to restore the table to its proper position.

The women, one of whom was a retired elementary school principal, had been commanding the table to rise on one leg and tap out answers to questions when, suddenly, it simply took off in a mind-boggling demonstration of levitation.

"We were all sitting in a circle," Wanda Sue said to me. "Our fingertips were resting lightly on top of the table, with our little fingers touching so we formed a physical-contact circle in which no one could have put her hand beneath the table to push it upward. Anyhow, it was far too heavy to be pushed up by two little girls or a bunch of frail old ladies."

What kinds of questions were the girls witnessing from the mouths of the prim, proper old women? They were trying to get tips on the winners of horses that would be running at Santa Anita race track so they could place bets with bookies.

Did it work? Wanda Sue didn't know, but said one of the women ended up buying an expensive beach house, so she got money from somewhere!

"Tell me what you know of levitation," Wanda Sue said.

I responded that I have heard of people who are able to levitate their own bodies, and fly around in the air while being investigated by a group of humans who are trying to determine if the levitator is a fake or whether he or she can actually levitate.

While in a room, one levitator was able to lift up from the floor and fly around, then pass through a partially open window, even though it would seem that the window opening would not accommodate the person's head and shoulders, but did.

Then he would fly around outside for a time before returning to the room.

The investigators would be in awe about what they saw and would make notes to give to the press.

Such reports often met with derision from readers who said levitation simply couldn't be done, but I had participated in pushing Wanda Sue through a window too small to accommodate her head and shoulders—under ordinary conditions.

I didn't know how to answer my friend's question about my opinion of levitation, so I said, "Being a student of one of the world's esoteric mystery schools—where you studied and practiced the mysteries of the universe which the exoteric world religions cannot supply their followers—equipped you to accomplish your feat."

"I couldn't have done it without you," she said. "You pushed my feet into the feat!"

This raises another question: Does it take two or more to tango on the cosmic plane?

Recharging Human Batteries

An indispensable fact is that energy is everywhere, and everything is energy.

Wanda Sue once asked me, "Myles, do you think that if people considered themselves to be rechargeable batteries we might live longer and be healthier?

I asked why she posed such a question, and she told me a story about her life in Missouri.

She had gone to Springfield, a city in the Ozark mountain area of Southwest Missouri, in 1988, when her father realized his incapacitation with Alzheimer's disease was reaching the point when he could no longer take care of her mother, who had never learned to drive, write checks or handle the kinds of business most women and men share equally today.

So Wanda Sue's parents, who had retired in Springfield in 1969, asked her to come there.

"I thought I was capable of meeting all challenges and facing them with mastery," my friend confided, "but I had no idea what I was getting into."

Apparently, everyone in the neighborhood had grown old together, so Wanda Sue wound up being the next-to-youngest person in an area where residents were well into their eighties, nineties, and even past one hundred—and still living in their own homes.

Although the topic wasn't discussed in over-the-fence conversations, most neighbors were waiting to die. And one by one they did.

"The old saying about things happening in threes was proven again and again," Wanda Sue told me. "The neighbors seemed to die three in a row, then a period of no deaths passed, followed by recycling of the three pattern.

"I began to notice that trees in certain yards suddenly turned brown, withered, and died for no apparent cause, and soon afterward a person living in the house where the dead trees were, died. In fact, the beautiful elm outside my folks' back door died at the same time Dad did.

The day after Dad's death in 1989, the tree let out a terrible rotten odor that was so foul I called a tree service and they reported it had rotted all the way through."

But the most profound effect my friend noticed was that her usual vital life force seemed all but gone. Her energy was drained, at times to the point she felt like she could only get around by crawling.

That's when she realized she was dying of others' impending deaths because her body, like a battery, was being drained so much it didn't have a chance to recharge.

She decided to try an experiment.

Tuning Up and Turning Back On

Driving around in the car, with the windows rolled up, Wanda Sue hummed. The generation of the hmmmmmmm and oommmmmm sounds activated her solar plexus and made her body buzz.

She then did more than hum. She shouted and sang at the top of her lungs.

"Observers may have thought I was nuts," she told me, "but I was desperate. I knew no one in Missouri, except my folks, to whom I couldn't really talk from the heart. I was lonely for my friends in California, with whom I'd had dozens of one-to-one, soul-sharing conversations. So I envisioned one friend at a time in the passenger seat."

As Wanda Sue drove around, she carried on one way conversations with the imaginary friend.

No one ever talked back, but an amazing thing happened.

A voice spoke to her with a profound message.

The Voice on the Radio

It was raining, literally pouring cats and dogs, and Wanda Sue was raining, too. She had been pouring our her heart to an invisible companion as she drove, saying she wasn't sure she could handle being caregiver to both her mother and dad, because it had quickly become obvious that her parents both suffered from different forms of dementia. And Wanda Sue found that caregiving, for which she was not trained, was a twenty-four-hour job that never gave her more than a few minutes' break.

Radio selections were limited. That evening, the only music on the car radio was country western, which was coming through the speaker with a loud, irritating, metallic twang.

Between the rain, the musical twang and Wanda Sue's own voice was a moment of clarity of consciousness that came as a thought: pull into a parking lot and wait out the storm or cause a serious accident.

She pulled into a Sears Roebuck lot.

The sky opened up more and rain, like a gully washer, came down in sheets that obscured her from anyone's vision. It was like a liquid curtain had been drawn around her, isolating her from the world.

"Suddenly the static on the radio cleared and a moment of profound peace entered the car," she told me. "Then a man's voice whispered with rich, resonant gentleness that not only sounded beautiful, it exuded love so powerful it filled me up.

"The voice said, 'You are a child of the universe, no less than the moon and stars…'

Wanda Sue later recognized it as a line from "Desiderata," a poem written by an anonymous poet, but at that moment she was so moved that all she could do was weep gut-wrenching sobs.

"It was as if the voice of God reminded me of who I am."

So said Wanda Sue, who turned around and drove home when the rain let up. She was revived enough to carry on with her caregiving.

As she pulled back onto the street, the twangy music came back on. Wanda Sue had not touched or turned the dial.

The incident inspired her to try another tactic to recharge her body's batteries the next time she was depleted.

The Testosterone Turn-on

The Sears store was located in a modern mall that featured a game room off the food court. There, teenagers congregated to play pinballs and other electronic games.

A loudspeaker added to the noise in the dark room that was filled with boys mostly between twelve and seventeen.

Wanda Sue deliberately wandered into the midst of a group of male juveniles, standing so near them she could feel their body warmth. She remained there, on the pretext of trying to see how the games operated, but she was actually experimenting to find out if she could absorb some of their energy, which was flowing heavily in the room.

"I stood directly beneath the overhead loudspeaker," Wanda Sue told me, "and felt the blasting of the rock and roll music, but I didn't merely listen. I let my whole body—every cell *become* the music by vibrating to the beats while, in secret, breathing in the air in which those testosterone-driven youths were operating."

She walked out recharged and rejuvenated, feeling as if she had a new lease on existence.

Old people had drained her of vitality, so she borrowed some from young people over-endowed with energy!

Astral Turn On

Wanda Sue found that her elderly aunt had cancer and her uncle was suffering from a debilitated condition brought on by diabetes. Both were in their late eighties, had no children, and asked Wanda Sue to also be their caregiver.

In her heart, she couldn't say no.

But the experience of four elders who relied solely on her nearly depleted Wanda Sue to the point she fell across her bed one Sunday afternoon in a state she described to me as a mental stupor.

"I was aware, but that's about it. My body was so wiped out I couldn't move a muscle."

Wanda Sue heard a voice whisper, "Yea, though you walk through the Valley of the Shadow of Death..."

The next thing she knew, she was out of the body and moving like a bolt of lightning that streaked from the middle of the country to San Francisco.

She was flying above a cable car, just as I flew over the sandy beach, face down and parallel to the ground, which, in her case, consisted of tracks descending a hill.

"I realized my psychic body's spinal column was flat against the overhead power line that provided the energy to the cable car in vast amounts of electricity," Wanda Sue said.

"The electricity went into my sympathetic nervous system and delivered a charge of such voltage to my body in Missouri that I leaped up, back in the body, recharged."

Bless My Soul!

"Bless my soul!" she said. "It must have saved my life." Wanda Sue believes she was truly on the verge of physical death and impersonally took energy from the closest source of tremendous power, which happened to be 1,800 miles from her physical body.

When she told me this story, Wanda Sue said, "I'm like the great singer Tony Bennett. I left my heart in San Francisco!"

However, her soul personality returned to Missouri to continue helping the older relatives she loved, a job that would continue for more than eight years.

Fortunately, Wanda Sue learned to protect herself against being drained constantly. One day a realization came to her that made it possible to keep going: I am in the center of the universe wherever I am. Universal energy is everywhere, to be accessed just as the sun's ray will be everywhere to be accessed if we can only realize it.

No one else has ever told me about being turned on by a cable car, but I've heard a lot of interesting stories.

Ultimate Power Trips

I know a person who has a terrible inferiority complex. He is like a little boy trapped in a man's body. He loves to hurt people mentally and physically because, when he does so, it makes him feel very powerful.

I observed him as he verbally put people down to the point that their physical bodies would be shaking or twitching.

Was he sucking or drawing the energy out of them and depleting them, and, at the same time, getting an energy high from the process?

It seemed to me that the situation was partly the fault of the victim, who participated and allowed the man to get away with what he was doing.

The person in question is a born again Christian who daily told others, regardless of their religious affiliation or beliefs, they were going to hell because they were not Christians.

He believed that he could do anything to others that he wished as long as, at the end of his life, he would ask for forgiveness from God and his slate would be wiped clean and everything forgiven.

In my opinion, this is one of the fallacies of many of today's organized religions. It encourages people to do wrong to others.

We will be forgiven for our errors, but they will not be forgotten, and our karma will be balanced over many lifetimes. A simple statement that holds great truth is "What we sow we will reap."

This person is paranoid because he thinks that everyone is out to get him. Because he believes that, he is finding out that it is true since it is being programmed into his subconscious.

What Goes Around Comes Around

After the man on the power trip beat his wife, he began to have serious marriage problems.

I have observed him over the years. His life is crumbling around him. I feel sorry for him because everywhere he goes he causes trouble for others.

He is meeting himself!

What goes around comes around.

I shudder when I think of the horror that awaits the man in this life, and later!

On the other side of the coin, there are people who go out of their way to help others. They also meet themselves, but what comes back to them is the good they gave others.

Mystics say: There is no middle ground; we are either backsliding or moving forward.

Meeting Ourselves

We can make great strides forward by helping others, or we can fall back.

From what I have learned during my OBE experiences, the souls on the astral plane want to return and meld with the Creator just as much as we do on the physical plane, but we have a distinct advantage they don't.

The souls on the astral plane have nothing to tempt them as do those on the physical plane, because everything there is pure energy and boundless love.

There, no one can kill or steal as here, so they cannot fall back or make great strides forward as we can, but on the physical in just one lifetime a soul can make so many serious mistakes as to be required to come back many times to make amends.

This is why souls on the higher planes sometimes admire a soul willing to incarnate on the Earth and risk so much.

Imagine the horrors that await a serial killer!

My Spiritual Quest

I have never met an OBE operator who is not on some kind of spiritual quest, whether through the path of religion, mysticism, or parapsychological pursuit for truth.

For many, as happened with me, the mystical "journey of a thousand miles that begins with but a single step" is kicked off when an individual has his or her first out-of-body experience.

I like the term Rosicrucian students of the mystical way use to refer to themselves as "walking question marks" because one automatically begins searching for answers to the question, "What happened to me?"

The adventure lies in the search for answers—which is the quest!

For example, I asked myself how Wanda Sue Parrott managed to get the keys out of her locked car. Was matter like plastic? Did it stretch when the need existed?

Do our own preconceived mental limitations prevent us from ascending above the limitations of the objective mind which equips us to live on the physical plane?

What do you, the reader, think?

Instead of drawing a conclusion which is concrete, here is my description of that remarkable event in the dark parking lot where my good friend proved every inch of her body fit through a space too small to accommodate even her head:

Being more than one hundred pounds heavier than Wanda Sue, and being a weight lifter at the gym, I simply picked her up like so much excess baggage and attempted to horizontally feed her through the car window.

At first it was a bit of a struggle, but then she seemed to ooze through the window.

Esoteric versus Exoteric Religious Views

The leader of an esoteric religious movement heard the story and simply said, "With God, all things are possible."

With God (the Creator) all things are possible.

This simple blanket statement is embraced by both the esoteric and exoteric religions, but the meaning may be quite different for both groups.

In esoteric religion, hidden (occult) truths are not only recognized, but many are understood.

When I look back on an event that occurred to my daughter's mother, I now know what took place.

In her early twenties she was in a hospital bed. She found herself at the ceiling near the corner of the room looking down at her body. She told me she was only dreaming.

However, she didn't understand the mechanics of out of body travel, which was exactly what she was doing.

During my spiritual quest I began to look back at my negative thinking and I would observe this thinking in others.

One friend of mine, who punched a time clock every day to go to work, told me that he would never be rich, by virtue of the fact that he had a low-paying job.

I responded to him by saying that he had sealed his own fate.

Even if he had said that in a joking way, the subconscious mind was accepting that statement as law and as a direct order.

The inner mind would then begin blocking money coming to him through various channels.

I told him to change his statement to a more positive one by saying that he has received all of God's abundance and is enjoying his wealth.

When I say he is enjoying his wealth it is because the subconscious does not understand the past or the future, but only the now.

If a person desires to be thinner he must say, "I am thin," but not "I will be thin."

If a person decides to be an actor he must say "I am an actor!" Immediately the inner mind goes into high gear setting up meetings with producers and other actors—it follows the order.

We are in effect creating our own reality for the better using "I am" as two of the most powerful words in the universe, instead of being an aimlessly drifting ship on the sea of life.

When Jesus said, "I am that I am," he was also using those powerful words.

When I see someone at work telling what an irritating person so and so is, then he is creating his reality in a negative way. We get what we expect.

It is better to say something nice about someone, or don't say anything at all.

If a person wakes up in the morning and believes that he will have a rotten day, the subconscious mind will arrange just that.

When a person says to himself that he is a brainless idiot then he is giving the inner consciousness a direct order. I have heard of people who continually said that who ended up with a brain tumor.

If an individual believes that he or she is ugly, then that person will begin to appear to others as being ugly because it will be expressed unconsciously through mannerisms and tone of voice.

Jesus once said, "Never condemn self or others because then you are condemning me."

I have had friends tell me that when they pass the age of seventy they will be wearing a hearing aid just like many other old men, and you can see what they are preparing for themselves.

Another man I met told me he would end up in a rest home like most other people.

I told him not to program that into his life since only a small percent of the people ever end up in a rest home; the rest live out their normal lives in apartments and houses.

I wonder how many people have died during hospital stays because their doctors told them they had only six months to live and they accepted that statement as law instead of believing in their own innate ability to heal themselves. This happened to a friend of mine.

The subconscious accepted the doctor's statement and arranged for her death because the patient refused to reject the death sentence.

The subconscious hears every little sound that occurs around us even if we overlook or don't hear it on a conscious level.

How many times has someone said something to us but we didn't hear them because we were busy at something?

Then a few minutes later the statement made by the person appears on our screen of objective consciousness because the inner consciousness decided that it would fit into our needs of the moment.

I heard of a lady who was told by her doctor that her gall bladder must come out immediately.

She did not accept his order as law, but instead began to take certain herbs which would bring about a healing.

Today she has a healthy, intact gall bladder!

At a later time a friend of mine was told by her doctor the same thing as the other lady—the gall bladder must come out. She accepted it as law because she believes that only doctors know anything about healing.

Today my friend has no gall bladder and she claims she is completely healthy.

I'm sure this organ has a definite function in the body or it would not be there.

Many of today's exoteric religious organizations do not, or cannot, teach us these mysteries. Sometime during my youth, I began to wonder: What am I doing here on this plane? Where did I come from? Where am I going? Thus began my spiritual quest. Eventually I found and became a student-member of the Rosicrucians.

Chapter 5

Going Hunting

When I was thirteen, my father bought me a thirty-two special Winchester rifle. He was always the game hunter, hunting mountain lions and rabbits in Big Tujunga Canyon. He also hunted deer and elk in other places. He thought I would follow in his footsteps.

On my first hunting trip, we went to the Lone Pine area in the High Sierras in California. We flew in from the main highway to Manachie Meadows.

After setting up camp, my father positioned me about halfway up a mountain called Round Mountain. The idea behind this was that the hunters in the valley below would be shooting at the deer, causing them to run up Round Mountain, where I would be waiting in ambush.

I waited.

Finally, a young buck with two pointer antlers came into sight. At a fifty-foot distance I put a bullet through his heart.

At that moment, the buck stopped in his tracks and turned his head toward me. He then began a slow walk toward me, stopping about six feet away.

He raised his head and looked me straight in the eyes.

His big brown eyes were beautiful and expressive. It was almost as if he said to me, "Why did you kill me? I meant you no harm."

Then his rear legs buckled, and next his front legs collapsed. As he lay on his side, he breathed one last breath. And he died.

I felt so bad that I never went hunting again.

I am sure the buck felt no pain because God, in His infinite wisdom, arranged for the animal kingdom a way for the animals to avoid pain.

When a tiger attacks a rodent and swats it around, and bites it, the consciousness of the victim projects out of the body to avoid pain.

However, the rodent still attempts to escape because of its strong desire to survive.

Do Black Bugs Bleed Black Blood?

After the hunting incident, I had acquired a healthy respect for animals, but not much for insects.

That soon changed.

Later, when I was living in an apartment in North Hollywood, California, I got up from bed around 2:00 A.M. to go to the rest room. I saw a giant water bug feeding on crumbs on the kitchen floor. I suppose one could really call it a cockroach; it was close to two inches long.

I promptly sprayed it, using a can of insect killer.

As I walked back down the long hallway to the bedroom, I looked back and saw the bug following me. As I got back in bed, I thought: How strange that the bug, half dead, would follow me.

At 2:00 A.M. it is so quiet one can literally hear a pin drop. I could hear the bug crawling across the carpetless floor. Then, it crawled up the bed post onto my mattress, not more than a foot from my face, and looked into my eyes.

It then fell back, dead, onto the floor,

I had an immediate flashback to the deer incident. The bug may as well have said, "Why did you kill me? I meant you no harm." The lesson I learned was one of respect and love.

All creatures large and small have the desire to live a full life.

All creatures must also eat—often each other—in the cause-and-effect chain of life.

Who Wants to Be Extinct?

As the white man headed West, he would shoot the American buffalo for sport or just for fun. At one time there were millions of these wonderful animals that were hunted only for food by the Indians, but they were killed almost to extinction by the white men.

Fortunately, the American bison was saved by concerned groups of people.

The passenger pigeon, unfortunately, became extinct in the eastern United States. At one time, in great numbers, passenger pigeons would darken the skies for as far as one could see.

Hunters from all over the world went to Africa to shoot elephants and rhinoceros, and to India to kill the tiger. In a few more years these animals will go the way of the passenger pigeon unless strict corrective measures are put into force.

Since animals can't speak, people must advocate for them by asking: Who wants his species to become extinct?

If you were asked that question, what would you say?

Can you imagine the Earth devoid of human beings?

Carcasses and Karma

In many cases where people are mauled or gored by animals, the question is raised, "Why me?"

Or, if an individual is killed, "Why him?"

When viewed from the philosophical perspective that nothing happens by chance, a question arises:

Is it possible the person attacked by an animal has, at one time or another—in this lifetime or a previous lifetime—tormented or killed animals for the sheer joy of doing so rather than from the need to eat?

An imaginary picture of human carcasses isn't very pleasant, yet human beings shot American buffalo and African rhinos by the dozens, leaving the carcasses of the beautiful animals to rot in the sun.

I heard of a case in which a doctor in a previous life worked with various animals in a laboratory setting, for experimental purposes. He sometimes cut off the male animals' testicles, causing them great pain.

In his next life, again as a doctor, he worked with similar animals for the same purposes.

He was bitten by one of the creatures and died from the resulting infection.

Can you see the karma working here?

Because more and more animals are becoming extinct, is it possible the people who have done all the killing will have to go to other planets which have a greater abundance of animals so they can work out their negative karma—or wait until some time in the future when the Earth is replenished again with more animals?

An old Chinese proverb states: Once gone, a species is gone forever so be careful whose beautiful, perfect life you destroy.

Animal Attacks

I have heard of several cases in which common house cats have allegedly been responsible for the deaths of infants because the babies' mothers paid more attention to their children than their pets.

While scientists, like the researchers into feline behavior at Tufts University, do not believe many such "old wives' tales," there are those who claim them to be true.

In one case, the mother found the family cat straddling the head and neck of her child. It appeared to be attempting to suck the air out of the baby's lungs to bring about suffocation.

Scientists claim cats may be trying to get tastes of the milk they smell on infants' breath, but no one knows what's in a cat's mind except the cat, so I say:

Consider the possible karmic implications for the infants who have been killed by cats.

Dogs kill humans, too. In a recent event in California, a pick-up truck driver saw a pit bull tossing around what the man thought was a rag doll, so he just drove on by. Later, when he saw the evening news on television, he realized his mistake. The rag doll was an 85-year-old woman who did not survive the attack.

Many owners of pit bulls who saw the news broadcast had their own pit bulls put to sleep out of fear for their own personal safety, or the possibility of being sued by those claiming their dogs hurt others.

A California woman was killed by a mountain lion as she jogged in a wooded area, although it is rare to hear of such a fatal attack in the area.

Going back to Edgar Cayce's statement that *nothing happens by chance* causes one to wonder.

I heard of a case in which a hunter in Africa was hunting cape buffalo, which are very dangerous animals. After firing a couple of rounds at a charging buffalo, the hunter panicked, dropped his rifle, and climbed a tree.

The wounded, enraged animal was able to rear up with his front hooves resting against the trunk of the tree, its snout touching the hunter's shoe.

The man could not climb any higher because of the shortness of the tree. The buffalo began to lick the hunter's shoe, continuing until—after a long time—the leather was licked away. The man bled to death.

The mortally wounded buffalo, its mission completed, died at the foot of the tree. They were found dead together.

Sounds like instant karma to me!

Did Man Dine With the Dinosaurs?

According to scientists the dinosaur perished about seventy million years ago. But something occurred a number of years ago in the southern United States to dispute the idea that man has only been here a few million years, namely five to ten million years.

A man's footprints were found in a river bed alongside the footprints of an allosaurus dinosaur predator. It appeared that the allosaurus was hunting or tracking the man.

If this is true then possibly man has been here a lot longer than previously thought.

One of the oldest complete skeletons of a human ever found was discovered in a foreign country of a man or woman buried under several hundred feet of coal. Coal is the remains of plants and animals. The person had died about ten million years ago and it took several million years for the forests to live and die over the body, with each added layer piling up.

I went to the tar pits in Los Angeles recently, and a worker there said the tar only goes down to forty or forty-five thousand years and then hits bedrock—but other parts, if there are any, may go lower.

I heard that a number of years ago a man's frozen body was found in a cave in the far north. With the man was found a camel and a mammoth elephant, both of which were small animals and probably were his pets. They were gathered around a fireplace.

The mammoth elephant became extinct about ten thousand years ago and this fact disputes any notion by modern religions that we humans have been here only four thousand years—a neat little package made up by someone.

The cave man appeared to be Aryan and the subsequent carbon dating of the area indicated that he probably froze to death forty-some thousand years ago, along with millions of other animals and humans who were in the region.

They all died within seconds because of the extreme cold brought on by the Pole Shift of 48,000 B.C. as psychic author Ruth Montgomery's guides attested. One mammoth found in the region was found with buttercup flowers in its mouth and it froze to death while chewing them. As Montgomery's guides claim, the next Pole Shift will occur at the end of this century.

More about Ruth Montgomery appears in other parts of this book. She claims that the South Pole will probably move off from Antarctica and if there are any scientists left alive they will go there and discover millions of carcasses of mammoths and other animals, along with some people, as they have in Siberia. The animals found in Siberia were the result of the Pole Shift in 48,000 B.C.

Karma and the Food Chain

The American Indians thanked their brothers and sisters in spirit for giving up their lives so the humans could eat to sustain their lives.

Did the Indians understand the food chain differently than we do? They hunted for food, not for fun.

What, if any, is the karmic implication of eating other life forms on the food chain? Many concerned people ask this question, especially as it applies to eating the flesh of animals.

Although I do not eat pork or red meat, my daily diet does include turkey, chicken and fish. After thinking about all that has been said about killing animals, the word "hypocrite" begins to loom in my mind.

How many turkeys, chickens, and fish die so I can fill my stomach? How many die to fill yours?

Nutritionally speaking, it is much more healthful to eat fish or fowl than to eat red meat, with its low vibratory rate.

Red-meat eaters have a much higher incidence of ulcers because, when the meat enters the stomach, twice as much hydrochloric acid is secreted to digest the red meat than for other food types.

It is probably better not to eat meat at all, but the person who embarks on a meatless diet runs the risk of developing a protein deficiency.

Before eliminating meat from one's diet, such a person should first learn to mix the proper foods to get sufficient protein.

If a person has been eating beef for a long time and quits "cold turkey," it is a shock to the system; such a dietary change should be done slowly.

Eating fruits, nuts,, vegetables and grains may be the better route to go.

When I eat grapes, I'm careful not to throw away any good ones, keeping in mind that each grape vine—with its harvest—has its own innate intelligence.

The purpose of each grape is to feed a human or an animal.

As far as meat is concerned, Edgar Cayce recommended fish, fowl, and, occasionally, lamb.

Cancer radicals have been found in chicken, but never in turkey; but, of course, one might get a little sleepy on turkey because it contains tryptophan, as do milk and lettuce.

Aw, Nuts!

When eating nuts, I prefer the raw, unsalted almonds.

I heard that Edgar Cayce claimed that eating three almonds a day would help a person to never get cancer because the nut contains laetrile, a natural cancer fighter. Laetrile is also found in lima beans and apricot seeds.

Alkaline Versus Acid

I prefer the almond and brazil nuts, which are alkaline, over other nuts, but never eat them salted or cooked. Most fruit is alkaline; however, plums and cranberry juice are not.

Most vegetables are alkaline, but corn is not.

For a little extra energy I use the ginseng herb. There is American, Siberian and Korean red ginseng.

For a good anti-oxidant I use grape seed extract called pycnogenol, which is reputed to be much stronger than vitamins C and E, also anti-oxidants.

Pycnogenol vacuums out the free radicals in my system, such as insecticides and lead. I definitely have a feeling of well-being from it. My seventy-five-year-old mother uses it and now works out in her garden. Before she didn't have the energy.

Is this karma in action, good sense or a bit of both?

Even plants have a consciousness, as people who talk and pray to their plants know.

Plants, Pain, and the Food Chain

A number of years ago scientists conducted a test on plants to determine if they had consciousness. They placed a plant in a room with an entry door and an exit door.

Then, they attached wires from the plant to a very sensitive machine that registered sound beyond the range of normal human hearing: in other words, sound that is inaudible to human ears.

They then brought a man into the room; he tore off one of the branches of the plant. The plant screamed, and the scream was registered on the sensitive machine.

Next, the scientists lined up ten men at the entry door, with the number-ten man being the person who had torn the branch from the plant.

The number-one man opened the entry door, walked past the plant, and exited through the exit door. The machine registered no sound. The next eight men—one at a time—passed the plant without incident.

When the number-ten man opened the entry door, the plant recognized him and screamed!

These ideas give us food for thought when we go hunting—if only for food someone else harvested so we can shop to suit ourselves at our local grocery store.

Chapter 6

War and Karma

EVEN THE EARTH HAS A CONSCIOUSNESS and, in fact, is a living organism.

According to Edgar Cayce, man has been on the planet for ten-and-a-half million years, in the physical body. Before that time, we were helping other souls in creating the physical universe. Some of us chose to enter into physical bodies, became trapped here, and, after a number of lifetimes, forgot where we came from. This was the first wave of souls. A second wave came down to try to bring us back, but some of them became trapped also. At the head of the second wave was Amilius, the same soul as the Master Jesus.

If one could condense the Earth's history into twenty-four hours, then man has been on the planet for only a few moments. In that time, he has nearly destroyed the planet by killing the animals, polluting the water and the air, and depleting natural resources—to say nothing of his inhumanity to his fellow man.

At different times in the history of man, great avatars/masters have appeared to bring light to the darkness of man's thinking. Buddha, Confucius, Mohammed, and others appeared at the darkest times of history. The greatest of these masters was Jesus.

One of his great statements of truth was: "Turn the other cheek." As an analogy, when a dog is about to be attacked by a much-larger dog, the smaller animal lies down on its back. In so doing, it avoids annihilation. At the same time, it triumphs over the larger dog because the victor always becomes the vanquished at a later time at the hands of another.

In the few million years that man has been on the planet, there have always been the victors and the vanquished in wars.

When an individual attacks another, or when a nation attacks another nation, they are setting traps for themselves. When Hitler's tanks rolled across France, France was the vanquished because in a previous time they had been the victors who had attacked another country.

Terrorism and Three Antichrists

I saw on the news that terrorists hit us in Saudi Arabia and possibly blew up one of our airliners here in America, both in 1996. Someone mentioned to me how awful it was that terrorists would kill Americans. I reminded him that we have attacked Grenada, Panama, Iraq, Libya, Iran, and Vietnam.

"We blew up an Iranian airliner," I said, "bombed and killed a relative of Libyan leader Khadafi, killed about 185,000 Iraqi soldiers and close to three million North Vietnamese and Chinese soldiers."

"Are you siding with the terrorists?" he asked.

"I am not saying we are wrong in our actions," I said, "but I ask: Is it any wonder that terrorists are hitting us?"

Nostradamus mentioned three Antichrists. The first was supposedly Napoleon, followed by Adolf Hitler. It will be interesting to see who the number three person will be.

Nostradamus called Hitler by the name "Hister," and Edgar Cayce used the correct spelling. Of course, Cayce was alive during the pinnacle of Hitler's power, but Nostradamus lived hundreds of years before. Nostradamus' writings were rather vague and were interpreted differently by the many people who scanned them. Cayce was much more explicit in his statements.

Mysterious Horseman in White

At one of the Edgar Cayce Bible study groups I attended, a discussion was held about the fact that during World

War I, at a certain time, the Germans were advancing rapidly against the Allies. According to the story, the cosmic forces (of God) decided to slow the Germans' advance.

An army of soldiers dressed in white uniforms, being led by a white horse bearing a rider in white, marched toward the German lines. All available firepower was brought to bear on the rider on horseback, but to no avail.

At that point, the Germans retreated in fear and told their commanders what had happened. Some believe it was a case of Divine intervention. What do you think?

To Fly or Not to Fly?

Returning again to the subject of terrorist activity in the United States, the question arises: Is it safe to fly?

If I were asked that question, I would say it is much safer to fly in an airliner than to drive an automobile. Only a few hundred people perish each year in air accidents, while about fifty thousand people die every year from automobile accidents.

In America, if people are uneasy about flying, then they should remember the auto death rate.

I feel sorry for the people on the Korean airliner that was shot down by a Russian fighter. According to the report I heard, the plane continued flying for about one hour before crashing into the ocean.

Man's Collective Payback

When North Vietnam attacked its southern neighbor and became victorious, the usual celebration and military parade followed.

The victors here will be the vanquished at another time, as history repeats itself over and over—the blind leading the blind. Of course, the governments force their young men to fight unless they have volunteer forces. The volunteer exacts a heavier payback because he had a choice not to fight.

About fifty-eight thousand of our men died in the Vietnam war. After our soldiers returned home at the end of the war, another seventy thousand committed suicide.

When collective man comes to the realization that what he does to his fellow man, he is in fact doing to himself, then possibly the wars will end.

Chapter 7

The Death Event

Some people spend their lives fearing the death event. When I was a young man, something happened to a friend of mine named Charlie that completely changed my view about death.

Charlie had gone to the doctor and received a shot of penicillin. Neither Charlie nor the doctor was aware that Charlie was allergic to penicillin. Upon returning home, Charlie became very ill and collapsed on the bedroom floor, although he was conscious of what was happening to him. According to Charlie, he felt the life force leaving his body.

It began from the fingertips and the tips of his toes, and began working its way upward. As the life force moved up his arms and legs, the areas behind it became completely numb. At this time Charlie emerged out of the top of his head with a loud, crackling, electrical sound.

Now that he was out of his body, Charlie found himself running through a field full of six-foot-high reeds that he said felt like velvet to the touch.

As he approached a river, he saw several people standing there in white robes, whom he recognized as his relatives and friends who had died during his younger years. He carried on a conversation with them for a time.

Meanwhile, back at the house, Charlie's mother discovered her son and immediately called the doctor, who raced to the house and examined the body. There was no pulse. He decided Charlie was dead, but gave him a shot of something that would counteract the penicillin in hopes it would bring Charlie's life back.

Meanwhile, back at the river, Charlie's deceased relatives were telling him that he was much too young to die and had a lot of work to do in his life, so he would not be able to join them.

At that moment, the doctor jammed the needle into Charlie's arm; he said he felt like a giant magnet was drawing him back to his body, away from his relatives whom he did not want to leave.

Charlie knew that once he was back in the body, he would feel pain, so he fought the pulling sensation. It was to no avail. He slipped back into his body with a thud.

Upon regaining consciousness, Charlie learned from the doctor that he had been dead for several minutes.

Then Charlie told his mother about the people at the river, but she was skeptical of the story. Perhaps Charlie's mother was skeptical about my friend's near-death experience (NDE) because people of our Western culture are fearful about the transition from physical to nonphysical life as a result of religious teachings. They promise eternal life in heaven or eternal damnation in hell, depending on whether the departed individual is judged good or bad.

Individual NDEs have been reported a lot lately. Less is written about collective near-death phenomena—or the collective experiences of groups of people faced with death together, or who all die at once in such cataclysms as earthquakes.

Because I live within a few miles of the 1994 Northridge earthquake in California, I was aware that many people lost their lives and thousands more feared for their lives.

Following the quake, five scientists on the television news claimed we would very likely have an earthquake such as that in Kobe, Japan, between Los Angeles International Airport and downtown Los Angeles within another three years.

Being a survivor of the 1971 Sylmar earthquake that also killed many people, I was very concerned about the scientists' prediction claiming they expected a monster quake because of the huge fault that runs from Laguna Beach to downtown Los Angeles.

Predictions of Disaster

Edgar Cayce long ago predicted that Los Angeles would suffer from a massive quake. Was the 1994 earthquake the Big One? Or is it yet to come?

Jeane Dixon, one of the few psychics who has credibility to her predictions, made one that I heeded. She claimed we would experience, in the Los Angeles area, a quake of the magnitude of the big one that hit Kobe, Japan, a few years ago; it would occur between March 2 and March 9 of the year in which she made the prediction.

The reason I took her statement seriously was because of a fellow postal employee. This friend was on a warship during the Vietnam conflict, at which time Jeane Dixon claimed his ship would be hit by a shore battery hidden on an island, the U.S. military being unaware of its presence. The time she predicted the vessel to be hit came and went, and my friend was transferred off the ship to another location. At that time, he figured the psychic didn't know what she was talking about.

Twelve months later, the ship was hit by the shore battery hidden on the island. Jeane Dixon was fulfilled one year late!

Between March 2 and March 9, I refused to exercise in the Encino, California, gym where I work out because, just directly above it, there is a parking lot that could collapse. If a quake hit and the parking lot collapsed, people below it could be killed.

Twelve months came and went without incident after the time of her prediction, except for several notable Northridge aftershocks. It is better to be safe than sorry. I am happy to report that I was safe!

Jeane Dixon had a reputation for being about eighty percent correct on her predictions. However, the fact that her prediction didn't come true in my case had no bearing on the effects I experienced from another earthquake.

Quakes at a Distance

A short time ago I flew to Crescent City, California, to see my mother. Crescent City is located on the coast just south of the Oregon border.

On my mother's seven acres of land are redwood trees one hundred feet high.

Back in 1964, my mother said, an 8.5-magnitude earthquake struck Anchorage, Alaska, lasting about seven minutes. It generated a tidal wave that crossed the Pacific Ocean and washed over the tops of several buildings, drowning many people in Crescent City.

On the second night of my recent visit at Mother's house, around 9:00 P.M., I felt the bed shake. I mentioned it to her, but my mother said she had felt nothing unusual.

The next morning the papers mentioned that the previous evening a 7.7 earthquake had struck Adak, Alaska, sending a small wave all the way to Crescent City, but it was too small to do any damage.

The fact that I felt an earthquake from such a distance seems strange; probably the ocean carried the vibrations to Crescent City in the way a copper wire carries electricity.

Animals are reputed to be able to predict quakes, perhaps by sensing tremors in the earth that humans aren't sensitive to because of our conditioning. Some people are more sensitive than others. In 1965 an earthquake registering 8.5 on the Richter scale occurred in South America. In 1977 one earthquake killed five hundred thousand people in China; another killed two hundred thousand in Guatemala the same year.

Seven hundred thousand died from quakes at approximately the same time. How many predicted the death event?

Is fear of death lessened when many others die at the same time? Or is every NDE an individual experience some fear and others don't?

I do my best to avoid disaster. But death—a natural event in everyone's life—isn't something I spend my life fearing.

Most people I know who are conscious of their out-of-body projections (OBEs) say the same thing: I lost my fear of death when I discovered a part of me cannot be destroyed.

Close Encounters with Death

My friend Charlie's close brush with death changed my view about death because he was one of the first persons who shared a personal out-of-body experience with me.

I knew he was telling the truth about his reactions to penicillin because I began having my own OBEs when I was just a child. Years later another friend shared her own experience with penicillin and the subsequent near death experience caused by her allergic reaction.

When Wanda Sue Parrott received a dose of penicillin at age twenty-six, she was unaware of her allergy to the drug. Shortly after getting a shot, she began having symptoms of a heart attack.

"I was alone in my apartment. My body began tingling from the outer extremities inward, with all sensations turning numb until my ears were buzzing and my vision was blanking out," she said. "My chest was being crushed. I couldn't breathe. Consciousness was the last thing to go.

I knew I was going to fall, but felt nothing when I did fall to the floor. Everything was like a sea of gray."

She lay in a sort of conscious state of suspended animation for a long time—which later proved to have been all night. Eventually, her sensations began returning and she heard voices that sounded like an invisible choir chanting: "Yea, though you walk through the Valley of the Shadow of Death, have no fear. We are here to comfort and to guide you. You are to go north and write a book...write a book...write a book..."

"I pulled myself from the floor and onto the bed," Wanda Sue said, "knowing it was time to leave Hollywood."

A few weeks later she moved to a town north of Los Angeles and began devoting every spare moment to writing. Today she has several published books.

"My near-death experience was the closest I ever came to actually feeling myself protected by a guardian angel," she told me, "but it wasn't just one such spiritual thing. It seemed I heard the voice of a whole choir of angels whose sweet sounds faded out as the material world faded back in."

Out-of-body projectors are eager to learn as much about life as possible. It takes near-death experiences to awaken many of us to the true meaning of the words "everlasting life." Special friendships develop between people who truly share their hearts and souls.

Another friend of mine, named Bill, was only twenty-one years old when he found out that his girlfriend had just died in an automobile accident. He was so upset that he decided to end his life.

Bill went into the bathroom and swallowed a bottle of his mother's sleeping pills. Shortly after that, he lost consciousness and collapsed on the bathroom floor, where his mother found him and called the ambulance.

Bill was taken to the hospital, where he was pronounced dead on the operating table. About that time, Bill felt himself slip out of his body. As he looked out the window, he decided to leave, but a voice told him sternly not to do so. Bill was at the corner of the operating room observing his body surrounded by doctors and nurses. He noticed that a long cord seemed to come out of the solar plexus area of his body and extend to himself.

This extension is called the Silver Cord; it extends from our physical body to us when we are out of the body at any given time. This cord will extend a great distance.

The doctors pounded on Bill's chest in an effort to revive him, and that is when he was pulled back into his body. As the doctors revived him, he was back in his body, even though he did not want to be because of the pain.

When Bill awakened, he told the doctors and nurses of their conversations among themselves. They replied, "How could you have heard that when you were dead?"

Later on in my life, my grandmother passed away. We had been very close. I was not able to attend the funeral because of circumstances beyond my control—a fact which bothered me for a long time. For about two years after that, my grandmother appeared to me in many dreams, always hugging me and letting me know that she was in a happy place and not to grieve.

In one dream of her, we were hugging. The top of her head, from the eyes up, was a transparent dome and I could see the blue sky and fluffy white clouds inside of the dome. It was a rather strange dream to have.

I have interpreted many of my own dreams, as well as those of others, with some success. My interpretation of the dream of the dome was that she was no longer in a physical body, but had become pure energy and could travel anywhere in the physical universe instantaneously.

After a while, all my dreams of Grandmother abruptly ended, possibly because she had reincarnated again to the Earth, or she had other work to complete on the astral planes.

Our Own Decision

After attending many of the Edgar Cayce conferences and Search for God study groups, I heard that no one goes through with a death event unless they make the decision to do so. Nothing happens by chance. When a group of people perish in a bus accident or airline crash they have chosen to do so for various reasons.

This is not difficult to understand when we realize that we reincarnate in groups with our friends as well as our enemies to work with our karma. We must learn to get along with our enemies as well as our friends.

Some people choose to die by police bullets to focus public attention on certain people who overstep their positions, thus bringing about good changes. Other people choose to die to focus attention on the inequalities of court systems and the lawyers involved. Many people are murdered because they themselves killed others in previous lifetimes.

People are dying from complications of Alzheimer's disease. A lady whom I know was diagnosed with it two years ago. She does not recognize me or her own husband. Although medical science has no cure for this disease, autopsies performed on the victims show excessive aluminum on the brain.

Aluminum is found in toothpaste, underarm deodorant, soft drink cans, pots and pans, etc. Some companies have already stopped making aluminum pots and pans because they realize that, if it is proven that aluminum is the cause of Alzheimer's, then they could get wiped out by lawsuits as some asbestos companies have because of the health hazards.

I have heard that aluminum is easily absorbed into the body and stays in the body for a long time. My dentist told me that the toothbrush does all the necessary work on the teeth—not the toothpaste—so I eliminated that. I use underarm deodorant that contains no aluminum and many products now say on their labels "contains no aluminum." After experimenting with deodorants of different ingredients and being told how badly I was stinking, I found that deodorants with baking soda among the ingredients worked about the best.

Chapter 8

Visions

IN MY EARLY THIRTIES, when beginning to take a nap, I slipped into the borderline state where the consciousness is between being awake and being in deep sleep. This state is where we have many of our psychic experiences.

I then saw a large square, like a window frame without the glass, which seemed to me like a window between the third dimension and the fourth dimension. As the frame moved toward me, it seemed to become larger, and I could see people on the other side of it—through it.

I saw soldiers in brightly colored uniforms walking single file up an ascending corridor of a castle that they were attacking. They were carrying on conversations among themselves. I had the distinct feeling that what I was witnessing were soldiers of a Crusader army attempting to recover the Holy Land around the thirteenth century.

What I think happened here is that I experienced a phenomenon called "extension of consciousness " in which the consciousness extends itself out from the body to anywhere in the world in the present or past.

If this was not the case, then I was viewing one of my past lives as a crusader/soldier, although I think extension of consciousness is probably the correct assumption.

Dreams and Visions

Psychologists claim everything that will ever happen to us will be experienced or played out in the dream state. But no one can be absolutely sure of a dream interpretation. A nightmare can sometimes be the result of the inner consciousness's decision to restore a bodily chemical imbalance.

While sleeping I have kicked chairs, coffee tables, and walls. One time when sleeping on a couch, I dreamed that I was riding a bicycle and wearing a funny hat. A man was running next to my bicycle and he was trying to grab the hat from my head. When I kicked at him with my dream-vision leg, my physical leg kicked out and broke an expensive glass vase sitting on the coffee table.

A friend of mine once broke his ankle while dreaming because he had kicked the wall. You may have had similar experiences.

OBE Visions

One of the most vivid, colorful out-of-body situations I remember was when I was about four years old and on the operating table having a tonsillectomy. Three nurses and a doctor had just put something on my face—probably an ether mask—and I was losing consciousness. I was kicking and punching while they restrained me.

The next thing that happened was that I seemed to be about ten feet above my body, high in the sky. My body looked like a sky diver falling and falling through a colorful spinning vortex.

Is it possible I projected from both my physical and psychic bodies and, in my astral body, was watching my psychic body fall toward my physical from a detached viewpoint?

In that same year my brother also had his tonsils removed. During a similar out-of-body event he saw hundreds of soldiers in a long line, many of whom were marching to their deaths.

He said he seemed to be standing about twenty feet to the side of the advancing soldiers. Considering the fact that this occurred in 1943, the scene would have had merit because of the time frame. Hitler was achieving victories in Europe during World War II!

Farewell Visions

I have heard of and read many cases in which the concerned mothers of young American soldiers left their bodies and projected over to the theaters of war. In some cases, a mother's psychic projection was seen by her son, and telepathic communication took place.

It is amazing in itself that the mothers were able to find their sons in a large geographic area.

Many American soldiers who survived the war did so because their parents and relatives prayed for them every day. In some cases, at the moment of death, the soldier/son would appear to the mother to convey a farewell.

Sex, Dreams, and Visions

I once awakened from a dream and found myself laughing out loud. In the dream, I was on a freeway where all of the automobiles were either male or female sex organs! I would observe a male organ going up the entrance ramp and a female one exceeding the speed limit.

I wanted to share this dream with readers and, at the same time, not be thought of as a pervert. After all, it came through my screen of consciousness but I did not consciously create it.

As ridiculous as this dream may seem, sex dreams are commonplace.

Possibly the higher self was demonstrating man's preoccupation with sex mentally and/or physically, which can be considered one of many root causes of some of mankind's problems. Or, possibly my dream was just a comedy because, in the eyes of the Creator, sex is not a sin or error any more than food is. Both are bodily appetites as long as one follows the law of moderation.

There are millions of women who are sexually frigid because—when they were young—their parents ingrained into their minds the idea that sex is a dirty, nasty thing.

Science has proven that anyone who denies himself or herself sex will experience a shortened life span and have possible mental problems. On the other end of this scale, an overindulgence in sex to the extreme in one lifetime can mean, according to information I heard at one of the Cayce seminars, that in a later life the person might be epileptic.

How Much Sex Is Safe?

I have read that the average couple has sex between two and three times per week with each session lasting six to eight minutes.

On one extreme end of the scale, some couples have no sex at all. On the other end are some who have sex every day and, God only knows, how many times.

When I was a boy and just learning the facts of life, kids used to tell dirty jokes. One of them went:

When I was young and in my prime
I had relations all the time.
But now I'm old; at ninety-three,
Six times a day's enough for me.

Do you believe it's possible? As I said, God only knows.

I once knew a married couple who both told me about their sex life. The man wanted to have sex every night and never wanted to miss a night. The woman, whom I would classify as average, did not want to indulge every night, so it reached a point where she would read a newspaper while he was performing, and he then would complain that he felt like an animal while she read the news. Ultimately, this was the main cause of their divorce.

Many men who get married probably do so because they want a steady sex partner, but unfortunately—in many cases—the novelty of the sex wears off in about three years. Then the man feels trapped in the relationship, especially if children are involved.

I have three friends—two males and one female—who come to mind in this discussion. The female is rather attractive, with a face similar to that of Elizabeth Taylor. One male is a stocky, big man. The other is a skinny black belt. Both men were infatuated with the lady and were attempting to curry her favor. Things came to a head one day when the two men beat each other to a pulp over the woman, but, fortunately, some people got between them and stopped the fight.

The irony is that both men have wives and children at home, and the lady has a husband but no children.

Sex! As a philosopher once said: "You can't live with it and you can't live without it."

Love may make the world go round, as romantics say, but sex makes the world interesting—even in dreams. One of the most spiritually oriented women I know admitted to me she had a sex dream that shocked her when she was awake.

During the course of a famous trial in which a former athlete was being tried for murdering his former wife and her friend, Wanda Sue Parrott dreamed she was making love to the accused in his jail cell.

"I never even met the man in person!" she told me.

She projects through her dream window, as I do through mine.

Soul Visions in 3-D History

At another time in my life, I had another experience when I slipped into the borderline consciousness and there was the same window. As the window grew larger, I could see a well-developed man with nothing but a loin cloth wrapped around his buttocks and front area. He was facing away from me, with long flowing hair down to his shoulders.

Directly in front of him was the most beautiful green, lush jungle setting I have ever seen, possibly comparing with the jungles of Borneo or New Zealand. About sixty feet from him, and facing him, was a beautiful girl.

They both ran toward each other and embraced and, at that moment, I realized that this man was me some sixty thousand years ago on the continent of Lemuria before it sank beneath the waves. Every time I think about it, I get an eerie feeling that some sixty thousand years from now, a future me may be viewing me as I write this book!

Chapter 9

Atlantis and Lemuria

Seeing oneself in a past life in a land that no longer exists happens to many people. It is eerie. It is also difficult to prove.

I was impressed by interesting things former journalist Ruth Montgomery included in her book, *The World Before* (a Fawcett Crest book, published by Ballantine Books; this edition was published by arrangement with Coward, McCann & Geohegan Inc.).

Montgomery, a psychic who believes her information came from spirit guides, says that some sixty thousand years ago a continent existed where the Atlantic Ocean is now; it was called Atlantis, and those living there were Atlanteans. According to Montgomery, the Atlanteans were, technologically, the most highly developed people in the world.

(Montgomery says that where the Pacific Ocean is now, there also existed a huge continent known as Lemuria.)

Montgomery says the Atlanteans utilized nature, using television, radio, and laser beams. They were, however, short in two areas in which the Lemurians excelled: religion and philosophy.

Montgomery compares Atlantis with modern America: long on inventions, with high living standards, but short on spiritual and philosophical pursuits.

Through attunement with her spirit guides, Montgomery claims to have received this information, as well:

Delegates from nations of the world met in conclaves in Atlantis to determine how to eliminate the greatest threats to humanity of that day: dinosaurs, mammoths, mastodons, and giant birds that were overrunning the earth. Even though modern science places humanity at later dates than when these beasts dominated the planet, Montgomery says man had to act or the human race might have been eliminated. Consequently, the first toxic gases were used by man—to fight the beasts.

The guides, says Montgomery, also discussed beings from outer space who were attracted to Atlantis because the Atlanteans were so inventive. These space people, she claims, taught the Atlanteans how to prepare a "giant crystal" that harnessed so much power that the beams radiating from its central core, with the rapidity of sound, could drive machines across the heavens and under the ocean.

On a hillside, Montgomery says, the Atlanteans found a vein of quartz sufficient in size to reflect the rays of both moon and sun. By cutting away the earth from all sides, facets were etched, so delicate they were capable of reflecting every ray.

Montgomery says that since nothing in the atmosphere was present to deflect the sun's pristine rays, the Atlanteans had continual use of the crystal at all times except during rainy periods.

She also discusses Atlantean-style transportation, using basket-like conveyances that were propelled by smaller crystals that captured solar energy and operated a mechanism no larger than a quart attached to each basket.

The baskets could hold between one and four people; they were wicker, woven from grasses. The Atlanteans were able to fly to their destinations. (They were lucky not to have to wait in line at the gas station!)

The threat of beasts forced the Atlanteans to live in walled cities; however, the Lemurians dwelled in caves or under the ground's surface.

Montgomery's work is meaningful in its message: When one species endangers all others, its time on Earth is limited. Let that be a warning for man, who is polluting the land, sea, and air—to the detriment of all other species today!

According to Ruth Montgomery, the earth shifted on its axis around 48,000 B.C. and the sea came "lashing and churning across low-lying Lemuria" and all parts but the higher ridges of what are today Easter Island, Tahiti, Polynesia, Hawaii, Australia, Borneo, and New Zealand slipped under the surface. Present-day California, then an eastern coastal area of the lost continent, became attached to the now-western U.S., which rose from the ocean bed.

Modern science attests to the fact the earth has had several ice ages and polar shifts. The guides of Ruth Montgomery said, "When that which had been torrid became frigid, and that which was once icebound from lack of sun became tropical, the dinosaurs, least prepared to adapt themselves to the sudden change of temperature, died by the tens of thousands, for their brains were the size of peanuts before they were shelled, and their great bodies lacked guidance or memory." Thus, they smothered, drowned, or sickened from unaccustomed heat and died, as did many other great hulks living in earth's waters, air, and land.

Well-preserved dinosaur fossils are still being unearthed in northern regions.

Lemuria had served as a checkrein on Atlantis. After Lemuria sank, Atlantis became the world's unchallenged leader, with Atlanteans issuing orders that other lands come under their dominion, according to Montgomery.

When resistance was encountered, they took the countries by force, just as countries still try to do today.

Maybe Montgomery impressed me by showing that "history does repeat itself." Her guides said the facets of the giant crystal could be directed at distant cities, even across great bodies of water, which could be exploded by this crystal force. The threat of its use reduced other countries into submission.

The Atlanteans looted America, Europe, and Africa, to name a few.

Then in 28,000 B.C., the Atlantean scientists had been revving up the power of the crystal to new heights, hoping to subdue the Asiatics halfway around the globe. On an awesome day, they were trying to send its rays directly through the earth to what is now China when the land exploded in a mighty blast, the greatest ever known on earth, and down went whole portions of the Atlantean continent, including the base of the scientific world where stood the mighty crystal.

This area is now called the Sargasso Sea and, according to Ruth Montgomery's guides, at the depth of the Sargasso Sea lies the mighty crystal. At certain periods when the sun and moon are in the right positions, the rays reactivate the crystal so that it interacts with the encasing carbon, making it a peril for ships and planes at those specific times.

The guides agree with Edgar Cayce that the explosion on Atlantis triggered the Biblical flood from which Noah and his family escaped by means of the ark, although there were many other people around the globe who also escaped.

The nuclear-type explosion was greater than that at Hiroshima by ten-hundred-thousand times. Such an explosion has never been seen on Earth before or since.

Flooding was rampant in Europe, as well as parts of the Americas and Africa, but was largely confined to the northern and western hemispheres.

Returning again to the 48,000-B.C. pole shift, Antarctica lay in the temperate zone for many millions of years and was overrun with wild beasts. But when Lemuria went into the sea, all beasts perished almost instantly on Antarctica, because the polar shift produced such frigid temperature that none could survive more than a few minutes, according to Ruth Montgomery's guides.

According to Ruth Montgomery, whose books were at their height of popularity during the "Psychic Seventies" in the U.S., mammoths with their flesh, skin, and hair intact have been dug up from the frozen ground of Northern Siberia. Since the flesh is still edible, these great beasts are proof that they were frozen instantaneously before decay and putrefaction could take place.

Today we have mastered a similar method of food preservation; it is popularly known as "flash freezing."

According to the theory put forth by Montgomery, when the North Pole moved up to its present position from South Africa, it left a layer of ice several thousand feet thick, which melted and left Lake Victoria and numerous other large lakes.

Today, the north magnetic pole is approximately 1,200 miles south of the geographic North Pole.

According to information given Ruth Montgomery via her spirit guides, there will be a pole shift around the end of this century.

Whether or not you believe in prophecy, I have given serious thought to important issues raised by Montgomery. This book was published in 1999, leaving us very little time to wonder where we will be—or if we will be—when A.D. 2000 arrives to usher in the new millennium.

Chapter 10

My UFO Encounters

Unseen forces are popular themes with movie makers these days. Such films as *The Day the Earth Stood Still, This Island Earth,* and *The X-Files* are favorites with many people, myself included.

Is it possible that the impact of these movies will be cushioned when mankind universally accepts the idea that extraterrestrials have been visiting our planet recently, and possibly for thousands of years?

Are you ready for the aliens? I am!

My Encounters Begin

I remember at the age of twelve I would go to the library and read up on everything I could find on UFOs (unidentified flying objects) and flying saucers.

It seems selfish of us to believe that God created only us on planet Earth in this vast universe. Comparing the Earth to the universe is like comparing a grain of sand to a vast beach.

Anyone who studies a particular subject begins to acquire knowledge on that subject and have experiences relating to it. Thus began some of my UFO encounters.

When I was twenty-five years old, I had an experience one evening in which I left my body. I found myself in my astral body, walking on a pebbly dirt path that felt crunchy to my feet.

The full moon was shining and I could see the path ahead end abruptly as it went down into a valley that was concealed in a fog. When I glanced to the right, I saw what would be termed a "flying saucer" in an area of bushes and small trees. The craft was dark in color and looked like two dishes inverted onto each other. It was about twenty-five to thirty feet in diameter, resting on tripod legs.

I then heard a hydraulic sound similar to the sound of a dump truck lifting a dumpster full of trash to empty it, only it was much quieter.

A lid—or hatch—slowly opened at the top of the craft, and I saw the form of an alien being emerging from inside. The alien was climbing a ladder. He stopped at a point where his waist was level with the top of the saucer.

He then began to survey the area, but when his eyes saw me—my astral body—he jerked as if startled. At this point he pulled out of his belt a cylinder-shaped object about eighteen inches long. He pointed it at me. An orange ball of flame emerged from the cylinder and floated toward me slowly.

The last thing I remember while in the astral body was the ball of flame approaching within four feet of my face. Then I must have returned to my physical body, although I may have remained longer because we usually don 't remember the entire out-of-body experience.

My interpretation of that event is that the alien thought he saw a human being in the physical and wanted to temporarily disable me; or, that he is millions of years ahead of us in his mentality, so that he knew I was there astrally and did not want someone to witness what he was doing there (possibly to gather dirt samples or plants).

This was my first encounter with an alien being that I am consciously aware of, although it is possible that prior to this incident I was taken aboard a spacecraft and physically examined. If so, the memory is locked in my subconscious and could be brought out under hypnosis.

More Personal Sightings

When I was forty-three, I was working as a security guard in Burbank, California on the graveyard shift. One morning around 3:00 A.M., I stepped inside a building to take a break. Of course, there were not many people in the building at that time of night. I sat down on a couch and went directly into the borderline state (the state between being awake and deep sleep). I left my body and went up through the roof of the building. Directly above me was a large saucer craft, probably 125 feet to 150 feet in diameter, with evenly spaced lights around its rim. It was dark in color. The occupants had probably been observing me for a time as I walked the grounds.

I don't know for sure whether I left my body on my own, or whether the aliens actually pulled me out of my body as has happened to many other people. I seemed to be suspended halfway between the building and the craft, not able to move in any direction.

That is when I saw a small group of people leave the craft and float down toward me. A woman about five feet, six inches tall—with long brown hair flowing down to her waist—floated to me with arms outstretched. As we embraced, I could see that there were four men behind her.

That is all I remember of that event; the embrace was the end of it. However, only under hypnosis would anyone be able to know whether I was taken aboard the craft. I have never been hypnotized.

The aliens looked no different from human beings, although in many other cases of encounters with humans, the aliens have been three-and-a-half feet tall, with large heads, large eyes in comparison to their bodies, and a slit for a mouth.

About one year after that event, I was working as a custodian in Burbank. About 9:15 P.M. I was walking back to my cleaning area after a break when I saw a large and brightly lit object traveling at a very high rate of speed, faster than any aircraft in possession of the United States (that I know of).

Being about one-third of the way to the top of the Burbank mountains, I had a clear view of the San Fernando Valley. The UFO in question did not exhibit flashing lights, but looked like a very large and steadily glowing white light.

It seemed to be approaching from the southern hemisphere, then abruptly slowed down as it passed over the Burbank Airport and Lockheed Aircraft Corporation. In doing so, it passed very near two small aircraft flying in the same area. The light from the UFO was about five times brighter than the lights of either of the two aircraft. No sooner had it slowed down than it accelerated to an unbelievable speed and followed the curvature of the Earth until it disappeared from view.

That evening, before I went to bed, I prayed to the Great Universal Mind or God Consciousness asking if I could be told the origin of this spacecraft, which was obviously under intelligent control. Later, in the dream state, I saw the word CANOPUS in large capital letters, which I promptly wrote down in my dream diary.

The next day I went to the library because I had decided that Canopus was either a star system or a galaxy. As it turned out, Canopus is a star system a few degrees south of the star Sirius, which is the brightest star in the heavens.

Unless my subconscious mind fabricated this information, then possibly it was good information. I don't remember ever hearing that word before.

What I think the spacecraft was doing was photographing or monitoring the Burbank Airport or Lockheed Aircraft Corporation where the famous SR-71 aircraft was developed. If anyone is familiar with the SR-71, they will know that this aircraft has reached speeds of four thousand miles per hour in the Earth's atmosphere, and at one time during the Chinese Revolution celebration it was sent over China.

The Chinese jets were scrambled to intercept it, but they could not deal with it because their jets had a ceiling of sixty-two thousand feet at a maximum speed of eighteen hundred miles per hour, while the Blackbird flew at ninety thousand feet and three thousand miles per hour.

The Chinese government was embarrassed, to say the least.

Government Secrets Unveiled

A number of years ago a group of people got together and were successful in passing legislation forcing the Carter administration to release information compiled on alien beings and their spacecraft.

Once anyone has seen the films and photos released by the government, they will never again doubt that we are not alone in the universe. In fact, it appears that we have been continuously observed by outer-space intelligence since the time of Atlantis and long before that.

Our Teeming Universe

Is the universe in fact teeming with life?

The average man today is so busy with his work and everyday life that he is not interested in whether there is other life out there in the universe. The probable truth is: if man were suddenly aware that we are being visited by outer-space intelligence, there might be chaos. The people would realize that our government is not all-powerful, and fear might become the order of the day.

There are hundreds of religions in the world today. Many or most of these religions would crumble as the news got out about space beings coming here. Many religions claim that UFOs and space beings are nothing more than the devil or demons. Some religions use scare tactics such as these to keep people in the dark and in fear so as to control them. They are told that they will not be allowed to go to Heaven unless they conform to the dictates of the church. However, no religion on the face of this planet, has this power. All religions are man-made and many are giant money-making businesses that get enormously fat on people's ignorance and narrow focus of mind.

Monitored By Aliens

I have a friend named John who told me that he has been monitored by a group of aliens for a long period of time.

One evening while John was reading in bed, with his pillows against his back and against the headboard so that he was in a semi-sitting position, he heard a whining sound such as one would hear machinery make, only very high pitched.

A small spacecraft passed through the wall and stopped next to his bed. Then a very small alien came out of the craft.

As ridiculous as this may sound, we must remember that some aliens might be millions of years in advance of us in technology and mental awareness. While humans generally only utilize one-tenth of the power of their minds, some aliens are apparently using a great deal more of theirs. Some seem to have mastered the ability to disassemble and reassemble the atoms in their physical bodies and their equipment, so as to have the ability to pass through solid objects.

Because of the variations of gravity and atmosphere on some planets, some aliens appear to be very small (in comparison to man). Others are quite large. God experiments with His creations. Dinosaurs are a mute testimony to that fact—and they are gone.

After the alien came out of the craft, John found that he was incapable of moving any part of his body. At this point, the alien performed a small surgical operation on John at a point between the biceps muscle and the forearm, directly opposite the elbow, implanting a monitoring device so that he could be located at any time. No scar or mark was left visible when the operation was performed.

The alien then re-entered his craft and, with a whining noise, exited through the opposite bedroom wall.

The last time I talked to John, he told me that the craft had returned. One evening while John was in his living room, seated on the sofa with his dog next to him, he heard a familiar whining sound. The dog ran yelping into the bedroom and hid under the bed.

The same craft as before entered through the south wall of the living room, passed very slowly through the living room, and then passed through the north wall.

There is no doubt in my mind that these particular aliens are monitoring other people besides John for their own reasons.

Encountering a Mother Ship

I once met a man who was returning on a flight from Las Vegas. He said he saw an enormous cigar-shaped craft about one thousand feet in length, with small saucer-shaped craft entering into it. The smaller craft were probably scout ships that travel in the Earth's atmosphere, and the larger cigar-shaped craft was the "mother ship" capable of traveling in deep outer space.

I think that if Atlantis had not been destroyed, today we would be traveling to other stars.

Insight into Aliens

Are there aliens among us now, living in most of the countries of the world, that look like us and dress like us? If they feel threatened, or for any other reason, are they are able to disassemble the atoms in their physical bodies? Can they disappear—leaving a pile of clothing on the ground?

This kind of situation seems to have been witnessed by many credible people. According to reports by witnesses, some aliens are able to leave their bodies on their planets and travel here, moving about among Earth's people without being seen. Or, they can cause themselves to be seen at will.

When Earth man reaches this stage in his evolution, will he no longer have to spend billions of dollars on spacecraft to travel to other systems?

Legends and Myths?

I have heard that there is a group of aliens who travel here from the Pleiades star system. They appear to be very similar to us in physical appearance. When they leave their planet, they travel out into space several million miles in their spacecraft. There, they disassemble the atoms in their physical bodies and their craft. They then travel instantaneously to within several million miles of the Earth's atmosphere in their craft without being seen by the naked eye or on radar.

Who can blame them for doing so? Our military of some country would shoot at them.

These aliens allegedly have a life span of up to eight hundred years.

According to stories in Biblical literature: Earth man, in the distant past, had a life span of several hundred years, but God saw that man was becoming too greedy and corrupt and so He shortened the life span, first to one hundred twenty, then to eighty, according to Edgar Cayce. The Biblical Moses lived several hundred years. Ruth Montgomery claimed that she lived one lifetime in Atlantis for about three hundred years.

Post-World-War-II Visitations

Ever since we dropped the first atomic bomb (1945), aliens appear to have been coming here in greater and greater numbers from all over the universe to observe us.

Some of the earlier Hollywood movies gave them a bad rap and said that they were here to conquer our planet. The truth is that it is the people of Earth who are killing each other off, not aliens who are killing us. Aliens appear to have advanced far beyond the killing field mentality that Earth people are in.

I believe it is possible that they have gone far beyond us in their spiritual development and evolutionary journey, and they are fully cognizant of the fact that they live in the physical universe and are governed by the laws of karma just the same as Earth people, and for that reason they will not go around killing people.

The aliens are no different from us in the sense that they eventually wish to return to, and have a reunion with, the Creator, although it may take aeons of time.

Telepathic Contact

In physical encounters with Earth's people, the aliens have reputedly conveyed messages telepathically, including the fact that they have lived here on Earth in previous lives.

When I jokingly ask someone what planet he or she is from, I am really asking a legitimate question.

According to scientists, the age of the Earth is about seven billion years. Members of the animal kingdom have been here hundreds of millions of years, while man, who believes himself separate from that kingdom, has only been here about ten or twelve million years.

We were in existence before the Earth was formed and we will be after its end. Our existence is comparable to a circle with no beginning and no end. If we had a beginning, then there would be an end.

Possibly we have been on other planets before the Earth was formed.

Five Alien Beings

I heard that an alien encounter occurred a number of years ago in a southern state when a truck driver was driving his rig late at night. He saw a bright light descending from the sky. It seemed to land not too far from the highway.

The man pulled over to the side and decided to investigate. After walking a short distance, he noticed a saucer craft with blinking lights resting on tripod legs.

At this point, five alien beings came out of the craft and began moving toward the truck driver.

A doctor who had been driving behind the truck had also pulled over when he saw the lights; he witnessed the event.

The truck driver was a big, burly man weighing well over three hundred pounds. When one of the aliens came up to him, he grabbed it and lifted it into the air. The alien's response was to strike the man and knock him down.

The truck driver later told the police, along with the doctor-witness, that when he lifted the creature it was like lifting a feather. He estimated the alien to be about thirty-five pounds and about three-and-a-half feet tall, but exhibiting great strength.

Lights in the Sky

In 1962 my former wife and I were at a drive-in movie theater in Burbank. As we watched the movie, my wife saw a light hovering over the power lines adjacent to the theater and pointed it out to me.

At first we thought it might be a light reflection on the windshield of the car, so we got out of the car to observe it. The object appeared to be elliptical or egg-shaped, about fifteen or twenty feet in length, with no flashing lights but one glowing white light.

As we watched the craft, its light went from bright to dark, as a rheostat would do in a home. Then, a minute later, the craft would reappear about twenty to twenty-five feet farther away from where it originally was, but still over the power line, with the light again becoming bright. The craft repeated this three times, and then we could no longer see it.

I have heard many times that alien craft are seen over power lines because they draw power from them.

At the present time there are many satellites orbiting the Earth. The last time I was in Arizona I sat down for about twenty minutes, observing the sky, which was very clear, and during that time I saw one satellite (man-made), and two meteors. The satellite always appears to travel slowly in a seemingly straight line, but in truth it is orbiting around the Earth.

During that twenty minutes I saw what I thought was another satellite as it moved slowly across the sky, but then it stopped for a couple of minutes and then moved off in another direction.

Someone told me that I was drinking alcohol (I don't drink) or that what I saw was a helicopter, but helicopters generally make a lot of racket and have flashing lights. This UFO was traveling at a very high altitude and was obviously under intelligent control.

Life on Mars

As this book was being written, NASA announced that a piece of rock found in Antarctica was from Mars and exhibited signs of simple, primitive life. A controversy arose as other scientists discounted this theory.

I asked myself why they picked Mars, instead of the possibility that the rock came from some of the trillions of other spheres out there in our Milky Way galaxy or the billions of other systems in space.

For years NASA denied there was any life on Mars, but they also said there was a rock, currently called the Face on Mars, which millions of Americans have already seen in published photos. Was Mars once inhabited on a vast scale, but no longer—unless they are living underground? Explorations of the Martian landscape begun in the summer of 1997 may resolve the issue that led to much speculation.

The truth is, according to myths and legends, that mining operations have been going on for thousands of years on Mars, and on the Earth's moon, by aliens.

According to stories I have heard and read—which you may be familiar with too—mining equipment has been found on the moon that is much more sophisticated than anything man is in possession of here on Earth.

For instance, one story says that when the astronauts landed on the moon and observed two alien spacecraft watching them, the radio transmission was blocked out—but not before it was picked up by several ham radio operators.

Many accusations of government cover-up have been in widespread circulation since the first UFO sightings caught the public's attention back in 1947.

Was there truth to such claims?

I think it's possible that the Martian rock announcement by NASA is the space agency's way of slowly admitting to the public that strange things have been going on, things of which too many people are aware for the government to attempt complete cover-ups.

Cattle Mutilations and Abductions

Cattle mutilations are nothing new, and have been going on for a long time.

I heard that one cattleman came out of his dwelling and saw an alien craft hovering over one of his cows with a green-colored tether attached to it and extending up to the craft. The man evidently surprised the aliens; they took off in haste with the cow in tow.

Did such phenomena give rise to the line in the nursery rhyme: the cow jumped over the moon?

Reports of human abductions are on the increase. Some people believe aliens are coming here from all over the universe because of an impending pole shift, and others believe aliens wish to bring us into a federation of planets.

The truth is that strange things are happening.

Anywhere there is a mystery, there are men and women who try to solve it.

My own experiences have given me no doubt whatsoever that the potential for life and intelligence is universal, but like others who are caught up in the mystery I cannot claim to know who the aliens are or where they originate. But I venture to say they may be more like us than they are different from us.

So, to understand the possible nature of aliens, let's first get to know who and what we are as human beings. Let's stop being aliens unto ourselves!

Our Triune Selves

All living people have three bodies: physical, astral, and soul bodies.

We are all familiar with the physical body. The psychic or astral body is the energy body that leaves during sleep and carries the consciousness with it; it can sometimes be seen by others. The soul consciousness body remains in the physical body between birth and death.

National Investigations Committee

I have studied findings of the National Investigations Committee on UFOs for many years. Frank Stranges, head of the organization, has spent four decades presenting controversial photos, films, and discussions that often boggle the mind. NICUFO is located at PO Box 73, Van Nuys, CA 91408-0073.

Although the authorities deny that there is a structure of a face seen on Mars and that there are alien craft coming here from all over the universe, millions of people have seen both. One can fool some of the people part of the time, but not all of the people all of the time. Roswell is an example.

We have heard for many years about buildings and hangars in New Mexico containing the bodies (under deep freeze) of extraterrestrials and a collection of crashed saucers, one of which is completely intact. This intact saucer was copied completely from the inside out and now the authorities have several of them which are flown and tested in an area known as Area 51 near Groom Lake. A major highway is nearby and thousands of people have seen these craft. Col. Philip Corso, retired Army officer in charge of the original X files at the Pentagon, confirmed many such rumors in his 1997 book, *The Day After Roswell.*

I have heard that a group of extraterrestrials is now helping American scientists in their projects as they did the Atlanteans before (see chapter 9). History repeats itself.

Do scientists and authorities in Area 51 in their arrogance think that the thousands of people who have seen these American saucers will not be believed when they tell others what they have seen?

At the present time, the British government is rumored to be in possession of 250 alien bodies. About a dozen of these bodies are ten to twelve feet tall. Remember, God experiments with his creations, with atmosphere and gravity playing their respective roles in their development.

The same situation exists over there as it does here, with the governments fearing that if the people find out that there are greater powers and forces than themselves that they will lose control of the people.

There are unseen forces behind the making of popular television programs and movies dealing with aliens from other worlds. The reason for this is because, when the average man on the street finally realizes that we are being visited, the panic factor will be lessened. The reason why the average man does not believe in the existence of alien beings is because he cannot see them with his own eyes.

This reminds me of the time a number of years ago when five Cal trans workers (California state highway workers) were being interviewed on the television news. They claimed that they saw a creature more than one hundred feet long in the Pacific Ocean as they worked on Highway One next to the California coast. They said that they estimated its size by comparing the individual size of seals swimming nearby. This creature had a physical description similar to the Loch Ness monster. They have been seen by hundreds of people including a German U-boat commander during World War II.

This creature is probably a pleisaurus, which died out seventy million years ago according to fossil records. Many people who saw the news program said the Cal trans workers were probably drinking alcohol or taking drugs.

The coelacanth fish, thought to be extinct for seventy million years, was discovered on the Pacific coast in the late 1940s. Several more have been found since then. In this case, the evidence is too indisputable for anyone to make accusations about alcohol or drugs.

Chapter 11

Dr. Frank E. Stranges

Will UFO historians of the future list the name of Dr. Frank E. Stranges under the categorical heading of "contactee," "crackpot," or "truthsayer"?

The enigmatic Dr. Stranges persistently and consistently cried "cover-up" for half a century, starting shortly after the alleged Roswell crash in the desert of New Mexico in July 1947 and continuing throughout five ensuing decades. My friend Wanda Sue Parrott first met Dr. Stranges in the early 1960s when, at the invitation of Bob Beck of the Hollywood Civil Air Patrol, she attended two flying saucer conventions in Southern California. She described him as "preaching the gospel of UFOs." I met him during the mid 1980s at a Friday night meeting he hosted in a rented building in Van Nuys, California. A colorful, affable, apparently sincere individual, the Reverend Stranges was still preaching the gospel of UFO reality and accusing the U.S. government of covering up the truth. Regardless of what history eventually concludes about his veracity, I believe Frank E. Stranges to be a player—even if proven to be a minor one—in the unfolding drama revolving around the question: Do aliens exist?

Judge for yourself.

The following information comes from the UFO journals which are published by the National Investigations Committee on UFOs, Dr. Stranges being the head of the organization and the author.

Along with his interest in UFOs, Dr, Stranges has for many years also been a Christian minister. Many consider him to be a bit more of the fundamentalist (traditional) persuasion than the ultra-modern, liberal (New Age) approach. He is a respected leader of crusades for Christianity while, at the same time, sustaining his deep belief in the reality of UFOs. Some of his views are shared in this chapter.

There are rumors involving the possibility that Adolf Hitler did escape before the fall of Berlin at the end of World War II. There are reports that for some time he resided at a monastery in Spain because of certain agreements that were made with the Roman Catholic

Church during the height of Hitler's reign in Europe. There are those who swear that Hitler is still living in several inaccessible areas of South America.

The late general and President of the U.S., Dwight D. Eisenhower, once stated that Hitler and Nazi propaganda chief Paul Joseph Goebbels had promised the German nation that he was about to come into possession of certain "miracle weapons" that would drive the Allies out of Europe.

During one of Dr. Stranges's visits to Germany after the war, he had the pleasure of speaking to several German citizens who had an "inside track" that verified the words of Eisenhower. They reiterated that Hitler was indeed about to come into possession of certain saucer-shaped craft.

Some of the secret weapons included a flying bomb with computer-controlled TV cameras controlled by pilots hundreds of miles away. There were also long-range jet bombers with thirteen-thousand-mile ranges, ram jets, jet fighters, and an SST capable of flying four times the speed of sound.

Intelligence reports reveal that plans for flying saucers were originally drawn up by German experts Shriver, Manermohl, and Miethe, along with the italian BelLonzo. They chose a wide-surface ring that rotated around a fixed, cupola-shaped cockpit. The craft could take off vertically. They launched the first successful disk on February 14,

1945. Within three minutes, they climbed to a tremendous altitude and attained speeds that staggered their own imaginations. The U.S. intelligence forces reported these things to officials in Washington, D.C., who suggested that the whole affair be kept quiet.

According to Dr. Stranges, long an advocate of the belief in a U.S. cover-up regarding UFOs, certain sources revealed a secret map showing how Hitler and Eva Braun escaped. The map was allegedly found under Hitler's bunker.

The information showed clearly that their escape route started from the bunker and escaped Berlin via a "hospital tank." They were taken to Templehof Airfield, where they were transferred to one of Germany's fastest jets and flown first to Denmark and then to Norway, both still firmly in German hands.

It is a well-known fact that at that time (1945), Argentina's dictator Juan Peron—who was then Hitler's admirer—sanctioned the purchase of huge tracts of land by the German officials in charge of these plans.

These German saucers are reported as being seen in South America even to this day.

In conclusion, as long as world governments maintain a closed mouth policy, the people of the world will never know the whole story, whether it is about Hitler's survival or the fabled "stranger at the Pentagon" introduced by Frank Stranges as Val Thor.

Dr. Stranges tells of a saucer-shaped craft that landed on the outskirts of Alexandria, Virginia. A lone figure descended from the craft and stepped down to the earth. The stranger got in a police car and was driven to the state line, where he was met by another police car and transported to the Pentagon. There he met the late President Dwight David Eisenhower, with then-Vice President Richard M. Nixon standing behind him.

According to Dr. Stranges, this stranger (Commander Valiant Thor) proposed to give them written information containing the secret of good health and long life for the people of the United States. The commander was informed that his information would be taken under advisement.

During the waiting period, the commander was the guest of our government and was housed under heavy guard at our own Pentagon near Washington, D.C.

The information was subsequently returned to the commander with the excuse that to implement these "gifts" would completely ruin the economy of the United States. In other words, thanks but no thanks.

The commander was kind enough to meet with Dr. Stranges at the Pentagon prior to the Christmas season in 1959. Following his three-year stay on our earth, he departed at 8:00 A.M. on March 16, 1960 and, according to Dr. Stranges, Commander Val Thor has maintained constant communication with him since March 16, 1961.

The following information comes from Dr. Stranges in his book *My Friend From Beyond Earth:*

On June 5, 1968, Dr. Stranges was contacted by Commander Val Thor, who instructed Stranges to meet him at the San Diego airport.

Upon arrival at the airport, Dr. Stranges was greeted warmly by Val. He ushered Frank to the parking lot where they got into a car and drove toward the Mexican border. After crossing the border, they drove for many miles south to San Felipe. There, they parked the car behind a restaurant, climbed over a few rocks, and found themselves walking along the beach out of sight of the restaurant and any prying eyes.

There, on the water, was a saucer-shaped vehicle. Dr. Stranges noticed a power boat tied to a rough mooring, and the waves were gently rocking the boat—but the spacecraft did not move. Dr. Stranges was informed later that the ship was equipped with a pencil-fine beam that, when fixed on any solid object, kept the ship from moving one degree from that "fixed" position.

After Frank was taken aboard the craft, Val and a lovely woman called "Teel" showed Dr. Stranges around the ship. Val said that he had met Bobby Kennedy, and his first impression of Bobby was that he was a very nervous and suspicious man, but that he was also a man who shouldn't be crossed politically. Val had warned Mr.

Kennedy to stay away from the political race that year, but to no avail.

Everybody aboard the ship assembled in a large room where the viewscope had tuned into a certain hotel (The Ambassador, to be exact) in Los Angeles, California. Tension grew as they saw Bobby walking through the crowd. According to Dr. Stranges, Val then said, "God help him!" Suddenly several shots rang out. Teel jumped up and said, "If only he had listened!"

Rosey Grier attempted to shield the body of Mr. Kennedy, but it was too late. He had been fatally shot.

Later, Dr. Stranges went into a bathroom aboard the ship and was quite embarrassed to note the absence of toilet tissue. Then he heard a voice within his mind, which he recognized as Val's, telling him to look to the right and find three buttons.

After the first button was pushed, there was a sensation of a warm wind like an air jet blowing beneath the seat. The process crystalized the waste matter and caused it to drop off. The second button produced another jet blast of pressure and temperature. The third button produced a fragrant substance, making Dr. Stranges feel washed, cleaned, powdered, and perfumed.

Dr. Stranges had the feeling that everyone aboard the spacecraft knew what had happened, and he says he was embarrassed.

Dr. Stranges also wrote about another strange incident that happened in 1947—the "Roswell Incident" in New Mexico, where a spacecraft crashed on a farmer's land. The craft, which was flying low, was experiencing mechanical problems. The occupants of the craft decided to use an ejection capsule, which they did, but they were flying much too low. The craft and the capsule crashed to the earth.

Many of the local residents came to the scene of the accident to view the wreckage, which was spread out over a large area. Some aliens were still strapped in the seats of the capsule, while others were on the ground. The military soon arrived and told the local residents to keep their mouths shut about the crash.

The doctor who performed an autopsy on one of the aliens was a member of an organized religion that claims there is no life on other planets. He believed the body was a product of crossbreeding created by the government.

The Roswell Incident remains one of the most famous and well-remembered incidents of this type that have occurred in the United States. In the early 1990s "Unsolved Mysteries" investigated the incident and broadcast it several times on TV.

Leaving Dr. Stranges and returning to the 1960s period, there was a news presentation on television one evening:

That day—in the early morning—a large object, on fire, was seen flying over Texas by many residents. The object was also observed on radar, and it appeared to be over one thousand feet in length and going toward California. As it passed over California, still on fire and at a much lower altitude, it was estimated to have crashed in the Pacific Ocean on the other side of San Clemente Island.

I never heard anything more about it. (The object in question, that made the news that day, was moving much too slow to be a meteor.)

In another incident about which Dr. Stranges wrote, a married couple was driving down a highway late at night in an area where there were no other people around. A spacecraft appeared and their car engine died.

When they got out of their car, a group of aliens approached them and took them aboard the craft. The aliens placed the woman on an operating table and inserted a ten-inch needle into her navel area, apparently testing her for pregnancy.

On the wall of the spacecraft the couple saw a map displaying the area of our solar system as seen from the aliens' planet in the Crab Nebula. The map also displayed some star systems the aliens visited frequently, and other star systems that were visited less often.

As the couple left the spacecraft, the aliens gave them a book that explained everything about where they came from; but, as they approached the car, the aliens took the book away from them, explaining that no human would ever believe them.

The husband and wife were later hypnotized separately. Each was able to recall the incident under hypnosis. Both told the same story.

Later, when the woman made a map of the area of our solar system as viewed from the aliens' planet, American scientists became interested. Soon, a movie was made of the incident. You may have seen the TV presentation of this true story, involving the experiences of Betty and Barney Hill. It was popularly known as "The Incident at Exeter."

Like the Roswell Incident, the Incident at Exeter remains one of the great unsolved mysteries of the twentieth century.

In 1997 a startling revelation was made by a retired U.S. Army officer who claims to have been in charge of the Roswell file. He was able to come forward with the truth after the Freedom of Information Act was passed, declassifying many previously top secret documents. The public was allowed to gain access to facts about the government's knowledge of aliens and their activity on Earth following World War II. In *The Day After Roswell* by Col. Philip J. Corso (Ret.) with William J. Birnes (Pocket Books), the former army intelligence officer recalls a 1947 meeting of top brass with President Harry S Truman in which the president, then not very popular, asked Secretary of Defense James Forrestal when the Americans would be told the truth about the crash at Roswell and the recovery of the alien delta-shaped craft and several aliens, one of which was allegedly shot as it tried to escape.

Adm. Roscoe Hillenkoetter, Central Intelligence Director, and Gen. Nathan Twining suggested that Gen. Twining report to the president after the Roswell material had been studied. In about three months, Gen. Twining told Truman, "It was almost beyond comprehension."

Col. Corso claimed it was like "nothing that could have come from this planet."

An elaborate plan was devised, Corso says. "It will be a case where the cover-up is the disclosure and the disclosure is the cover-up. Deny everything but let public sentiment take its course. Let skepticism do its part for us until the truth becomes common acceptance."

Is it possible that Dr. Frank E. Stranges fell into this secret plan and thus became branded as a crackpot while, in truth, he was the first and foremost space-age patsy?

Chapter 12

More About Voices

When I was around thirty years old, I was reading about how the Biblical character Lazarus died and Jesus told him to come out of the burial cave. At that moment, I heard a voice say, "You were Lazarus."

I thought about it for a couple of days. I had feelings of "Wow! I was Lazarus!" on one end of the scale and feeling like "What a joke this is!" on the other end.

One evening I sat alone in a quiet place and asked my Higher Self if I was truly Lazarus, and a voice said, "Yes. The information has already been given to you."

I do not believe that I was Lazarus because I've known other people who thought they were Lazarus, or Peter the Disciple, or King Solomon. I also know that voices and dreams come from many levels of consciousness. Some of these voices are negative forces.

Jesus said, "There are many mansions in my Father's house." In other words: there are many levels of human (and possibly other-than-human) consciousness.

Lazarus, who rose from the dead, may be symbolic of any man or woman who achieves a new, higher, fuller consciousness of the many levels of light in existence. Lazarus may be symbolic of the soul personality that, having "risen from the dead," is now on the Path to Enlightenment.

There are many individuals who believe that there are souls who are "earthbound" because they did bad things while in the physical body. They are trapped here after death for long periods of time instead of going to the higher planes between earth lives.

When I was about thirty-three years of age, I lay down on the bed—face down—to take a nap one late afternoon. I went into the borderline state, or so it seemed. Although I was face down on the bed, I was viewing the paintings on the wall behind me, and all the furniture. It was almost as though I had eyes in the back of my head, but I was not able to move my physical body at that point.

There was a woman's voice in the room with me; it was close to the ceiling, but it did not stay in one area. The voice was moving around. Although I could not see a form where the voice was coming from as it moved around near the ceiling, I could see the area. She was mumbling to herself.

I asked, "Who are you?"

She answered, "I am Marie Antoinette."

"Where did you come from?" I then asked.

At this point, her voice came down from the ceiling to my right ear, still mumbling, but the event ended there.

Queen Marie Antoinette was in power in France before the French Revolution. When the people were starving and begging for bread, she said, "Let them eat cake!" She later paid with her life. I don't believe, however, that the voice was that of Marie Antoinette; I think it was just an earthbound soul playing games with me.

I don't know why the voice came down to my right ear unless she was attempting to slip into my physical body. There are people who believe this can happen; it is called "possession." Others do not believe true possession can occur; however, momentary "assumption" of one personality by another is believed to be possible, during which times exchanges of information—or even healings—can occur.

By sharing these intimate, true personal experiences I hope to inspire readers to open their minds to infinite possibility—not to give hard-and-fast answers to some of the mysterious phenomena I've gone through on my journey toward the light.

I have heard that people who die from alcoholism can be earthbound because the desire for, and the strong pull of, the alcohol holds them earthbound, as some believe it does also to tobacco addicts—smokers.

I've heard it said that an earthbound alcoholic will look around for living people who are drinking and, when he finds them, he will enter through the top of the head of the person doing the drinking and slip into his body in order to enjoy the aroma and taste of the alcohol.

At the time of the Marie Antoinette incident, I had not been drinking alcohol, although I did occasionally take a drink. I never drank again after age thirty-seven.

A few weeks after the Marie Antoinette incident, a similar experience occurred. I was working as a self-employed janitor in a downtown Los Angeles office building. I lay down on a couch to take a quick nap. The couch had three separate removable cushions, and I was lying on two of the three.

I went into the borderline state and there were the voices of two women moving around in the room in a manner similar to that of the Marie Antoinette entity. One of the voices came down to my right ear and mumbled something, and the other came down and, I guess I would say, sat down on the third cushion on which I was not lying. At that point, the feeling I had was that a hundred-pound lady was sitting down next to me, and I felt myself sink slightly into the couch .

This raises a question that science is still investigating. Does soul—or the vital life force—have substance and weight? I have heard that when a person dies—if he or she is weighed on a scale before the moment of death and shortly after death—the physical body will have lost a slight amount of weight after the departure of the soul, probably less than a pound.

So, I cannot explain the couch sinking in. Can you?

When I was thirty-five years old I took a trip from Los Angeles to Fresno, California, to see my uncle. Maurice would sit in his chair and smoke four or five packs of cigarettes per day and drink a lot of alcohol. My Uncle Maurice was a veteran of World War II; he had been badly injured in both legs, although he could still walk. For years he used prescription pain killers because of his legs. After that, he substituted alcohol.

Uncle Maurice would say to me, "I'm proud to be a veteran. And you watch: I will die on Veterans Day." Veterans Day was his favorite day of the year.

I went back to Los Angeles wondering about what he had said about dying on Veterans Day. Approximately two weeks before Veterans Day I had a dream in which I saw VETERANS DAY in capital red letters, which I promptly recorded in my dream diary.

Two weeks later, on Veterans Day, Maurice was found dead in his favorite chair.

I returned to Fresno to be present at his funeral. While viewing his body in the open casket, I had the distinct feeling that Maurice was standing next to me and attending his own funeral.

A couple of nights after I returned home, I went to bed and slipped into the borderline state. All of a sudden it sounded like a million bees were buzzing in my bedroom.

I have heard that when a person thinks he hears bees buzzing, it is actually a form of energy that is released when a departed soul is attempting to contact a living person. Maurice, an alcoholic, was possibly earthbound, and I felt that he was in the room with me. I don't understand why he didn't talk to me, or possibly make himself visible. Maurice did appear to me in a few dreams, and he looked very healthy. I think that is the way he wanted me to think of him.

Maurice confided in me while he was alive. He once said he would find God after death, but I felt that he wouldn't find God because—in all my years of the study of metaphysics and the mysteries of the universe—I have never heard of anyone dying and going to the astral planes to find God as a single entity or as a God sitting on a throne judging people.

In reality, after death we judge ourselves. Or, to word it better, we contemplate or go over the life we just had and look at the good points and bad points, and prepare for the next life to work with our karma.

To me: God is like a force that permeates anything and everything—the flowers, the trees, the good and the bad people—everything.

Jesus said, "The Kingdom of Heaven is within you."

If there are a thousand thrones in Heaven, He never sits on one.

God gave us a will so we could make our own choices, good or bad.

God is no respecter of persons because of their wealth or power.

God is a respecter of persons who help others and who do good deeds, big or small.

In one of my most recent experiences a strange thing happened to me in the dead of night about 4:00 A.M. I had gotten up to go to the bathroom, which I have always done at least three times every night as far back as I can remember. As I was attempting to go back to sleep lying on my stomach, I felt a weight pushing me down into the bed. I was startled and attempted to get up. I could not because I was in the borderline state and could not move.

Then I heard a voice saying, "This is Joe and I have come to tell you something very important."

I had known for many years that this was highly irregular for Joe to visit me in this fashion, when I was face down and he was behind me.

He continued by saying, "I am going to show you the effect that fear can have on you as it did me. Call me within the next sixty days and I will explain it to you."

With that I began to feel the weight lift up and off from me. After I was able to move, I looked behind, but no one was there.

In the next sixty days I found out that Joe was out of the state and hadn't left a phone number. After thinking about it I realized that Joe is not a New Age thinker and not a mystical type of person and in fact frowns on things of that nature.

Once when I was in a market and another time on the street I heard my aunt yell, "Myles," but when I turned around she was not there. When I asked her about it she responded by saying that she knew nothing of it.

At that point I realized that she knew nothing about attempting to contact me on a waking conscious level but that some part of her inner being had done so. I then knew that Joe probably would not know on a conscious level that he had contacted me.

Six months later when I saw Joe, I was careful not to ask him if he had left his body and contacted me because he would think I had a screw loose in my head. Instead I told him I had a dream of him telling me about fear. He responded by saying he knew nothing of it.

What did he mean about fear?

Joe had a triple bypass operation because of clogged arteries possibly caused by a combination of fear, fatty diet, and stress. When I visited a major hospital, there was a chart on the wall stating that the biggest cause of heart attacks in America is red meat and dairy products. Also, scientists had conducted tests on two groups of rats, both of which were fed the same food. The scientists would shake the cage of one group and stress them out while the other cage was left alone. The stressed rats developed clogged arteries.

So possibly fear would be a form of stress. But what did fear have to do with me?

I remembered that I had gone to several different Edgar Cayce Bible study meetings and I had heard there that shortly after the year 1900, Cayce predicted that Hitler would die in 1945, we would find the Dead Sea Scrolls in 1947, and America would harness the laser beam in 1959. Later Kennedy would be assassinated and we would land on the moon. Then between 1992 and 1998 Los Angeles would be inundated with water. I heard that when Mount Vesuvius erupts that within ninety days after that the Southern California coast would begin to sink a few inches per day, causing the biggest traffic jam in history or people heading east to escape from Los Angeles. A straight line from Salt Lake City, Utah, to Southern Nevada would eventually be reached by ocean water, but no one would drown or be killed because it would take a long time to occur. Only those refusing to leave would perish.

This is why people joke about Arizona becoming beachfront property.

Because of these predictions and also because I was only five miles from the epicenter of the disastrous 1994 Northridge, California, earthquake, I may have developed a fear or concern over these events. I heard at the Cayce meetings that people born in Southern California (myself in Glendale) were Atlanteans in former lifetimes. They would be involved in the California cataclysm for karmic reasons because the Atlanteans were greedy for power and attempted to conquer and manipulate the other countries of the world.

Edgar Cayce also said that World War III might occur in 1999, a pole shift would occur around 1998, and New York City would be destroyed by a bomb or earthquake in the year 2001. However, in some of his other readings, these terrible events may be lessened or not occur. As I write this, it is July 1998.

Returning to the occasion when I heard a voice say I was Lazarus, I wrote a letter to Ruth Montgomery in 1986 because she had been closely identified with Lazarus in a former life. Ruth answered my letter and said that many people have claimed to be Lazarus as well as Martha and Mary. She also said that it sounded to her as if I did have an encounter with a spaceship (chapter 10).

I heard at one of the Cayce Bible study meetings that Cayce knew six individuals who claimed to have been the Apostle Peter during the time of Jesus, so he invited them all to dinner. None of the six knew each other. You can imagine what occurred at the dinner table.

We should all learn to pray and meditate. Praying is asking God (however one conceives him to be) something and meditating is listening for answers.

We should learn to use our reason because sometimes a voice can be a negative force and should not be acted upon if it seems to be non-constructive or destructive. Remember, voices can come from many levels of consciousness. Using a Ouija board can be dangerous because the user can open himself up to whomever or whatever is in the area.

One time I saw on the news where an airliner had gone down and killed many people. A short time later, I purchased an airline ticket from Burbank, California, to Phoenix, Arizona. On the morning of the day I was to leave, I heard a female voice say to me, "This is your last day on earth."

This voice that I heard was some part of my inner consciousness that loves me and was telling me to cancel the trip. I had to think awhile and determine what to do.

Our objective mind (thinking mind) is equipped to deal with physical reality or our everyday affairs while some aspects of our inner consciousness are not. However, I did make the trip safely.

I heard about a man who was preparing to board an airliner when he looked at the plane and saw that it was completely black in color and enveloped in a black haze. He did not board the airliner. The plane crashed that day and everyone aboard perished.

A thing to remember is that if we hear a voice which we conceive to be a negative force, then we should say "I love you" to the voice. One statement of "I love you" will scatter many negative statements in all directions because love is the most powerful force in the universe. Love is a positive statement that repels negative statements.

Once my mother ate a hamburger that she had bought at a fast-food outlet. The small piece of beef in the burger had been out in the open air too long or had not been properly refrigerated, and she became very ill. She crawled around on the floor for two days before someone found her and got her into the hospital.

After a couple of weeks, she was released. I was able to visit her at home as she was recuperating, and then I went home. After I got there, I heard another female voice say to me, "She is never going to make it."

About the same time, my mother woke up one morning to see a beautiful being of light standing at the foot of her bed for a couple of minutes. There was no exchange of words, but she sensed a feeling of love coming from the being.

The voice I heard was incorrect, because my mother completely recovered. Or the voice may have been correct, but because of our prayers and the being of light, she was healed.

One interesting thing about my mother was that, before she saw the being of light, she was a little skeptical about my encounters with the light, but now she isn't.

My daughter's mother (my ex-wife) was a little doubtful about my encounters with the light and UFOs until a strange thing happened to her in Redding, California.

My ex and two friends were driving home in her vehicle on a back road that seldom sees traffic. About 6:00 P.M., far ahead and above them, they could see a large object with lights of different colors. The object began to move toward them until it was directly above their car. They stopped and got out of the car and looked directly above at the object, which appeared to be about two hundred feet in diameter. In a very short time, the object accelerated straight up into the sky and disappeared from view without making a sound.

Chapter 13

More on the Death Experience

A number of years ago, my friend Ben and I went somewhere on a Saturday afternoon. Late that afternoon, I left Ben at his apartment .

Monday morning Ben did not make it to work, so his secretary went to his apartment. She found his front door unlocked. When she went into the bedroom, there was Ben in a half-sitting position on the bed with his head and back against the headboard and a smile on his face.

She asked Ben why he didn't go to work, but got no answer. Upon closer investigation, she realized that Ben was dead. He had died sometime between Saturday night and Monday morning.

I think that when we die—or are about to die—our relatives and/or friends on the astral planes are alerted and they come to the person on his deathbed. At the moment of Ben's death, I think that he was talking to his dead relatives next to his bed and he was happy about it; thus the smile frozen on his face. Ben's relatives and/or friends were his guides to the astral planes.

Suicide, Karma, and Disease

My thirty-three year old late son-in-law was diagnosed with Lou Gehrig's disease (ALS), also called lateral sclerosis. This is one of the conditions widely publicized through the annual Labor Day telethons through which Jerry Lewis raises millions of dollars for research into muscular dystrophy and similar diseases. The term "Jerry's Kids" has become popular during the several decades that the telethon has been broadcast. It has highlighted the Labor Day weekends of millions of Americans who wonder whether such conditions as ALS are inherited or acquired.

Lou Gehrig's disease, so named because the beloved baseball star died from it, is not an inherited disease. Nor is it caused by improper nutrition. It is not contagious.

I learned that Edgar Cayce once gave a reading for a patient suffering from ALS, stating it was karmic in nature, the effect being the disease in one's present life and the cause originating in a previous life.

Most victims of ALS slowly lose their lives from one to ten years after diagnosis. The use of one's muscles fades out in time, with the victim ultimately not able to control bowel or urinary functions. At the tail end of the disease, the victim has only two remaining muscles functioning: eye muscles, which usually function normally, and the thinking process, which remains intact. The victim finally dies by drowning, because the lungs fill with fluid.

To date, many believe an orthodox medical cure has not been found; therefore, most people look upon ALS as always fatal.

Death-Defying Cure, or Quackery?

I have another friend who was diagnosed with ALS when he was fifty-two years old, but who was seventy-four years of age (in 1996). Why was my seventy-four-year-old friend still alive after nearly twenty-two years?

He said it was because he had his own bees and allowed himself to be stung every day. The bee venom does not cure the disease, but it stops it from progressing. Thousands of victims have successfully used this method of treatment.

My daughter's husband with ALS refused to cooperate when I tried to set up a meeting of the two men so that he too could begin bee-sting therapy. The thirty-three-year-old decided that only doctors know how to heal. The idea of being stung didn't sit too well with him.

Karmic Questions

When orthodox medicine did not help my son-in-law, he arranged with his doctor to starve himself to death by not eating and only drinking fluids, in order to avoid the final outcome of the disease. After approximately two months of self-imposed starvation, he died in 1996 after suffering with the degenerative disease for slightly more than two years, during which time his debilitation had progressed rapidly.

His choice raises a question about suicide and its karmic consequences.

We have all heard of cases in which people have committed suicide because of broken relationships or financial ruin.

People who die normal deaths are reputed to usually see their dead relatives and friends, ready to guide them on their new journey, when they leave their bodies through death and have completed their missions on planet Earth, but the question arises about the suicide case:

Has the individual who committed suicide made a serious mistake because he or she has not completed the work he or she set out to do?

Waking Up on the Other Side

After waking up on the other side, does the suicide victim realize with deep regret that he or she has made a mistake?

Does that soul personality set about planning for his or her next life so that he or she can begin where he or she left off?

According to theories proposed by people like Edgar Cayce, sometimes—depending on the gravity of the error—the person may be required to live several lifetimes to balance his or her karma for that one mistake.

But is suicide always a mistake?

I have heard that when a person is suffering from a problem and he is able to work through it, he will emerge a stronger individual. However, if one commits suicide, then as soon as he passes over to the other side, the problem he was going through is intensified up to a hundred times of what it was.

A Great Lesson

Once when my friend Wanda Sue Parrott was overwhelmed with problems she didn't know how to resolve, she cried out, "Just let me die!"

Actually, it was a wish to be relieved of heavy responsibility, she told me, not a true death wish. She reviewed the amazing experience that turned into a profound lesson: Her wish was granted.

Suddenly Wanda Sue found herself projected above her body on the bed. But she didn't simply hover near the ceiling, as many projectors do, gazing at her physical form.

The lesson she learned was that no one can escape from that which one carries in the soul. We may shed the body, but mind goes with us. The spiritual essence of Self is indestructible.

Following her conscious realization and acceptance of this truth, Wanda Sue heard a voice that seemed to enshroud her as it came from everywhere, yet appeared to be addressing her intimately.

The voice was powerful but gentle. It sounded to her like a man's voice, but she saw no one resembling a mortal male. Therefore, she describes the voice as coming from an immortal male. It said:

"You may now proceed forward into the condition called Death by men, or you may return to the body from which you have just come, retaining full memory of who you were before this moment.

"If you choose to proceed into Death, you must be reborn in a new body, without memory of the lessons you have learned thus far, and each must be repeated."

In that moment, Wanda Sue made her choice—to return to her present body, with its brain storehouse containing impressions that could be recalled as memories.

As she told the story to me, Wanda Sue said, "Myles, that was my first major decision, because for the first time in my life I decided to face my challenges and learn to take responsibility."

Back from Death

Wanda Sue suddenly returned to her body. Back from death's door, she lay in bed and willed her body to start functioning again, because—with cessation of life—she felt nothing.

Because she was not breathing, Wanda Sue willed her muscles to work to carry her through the dark house into the bathroom.

"I was able to see in the dark," she said. "I bent over the sink and splashed water on my face. Then I gulped water from the faucet. When I swallowed, I started to breathe again. All the pain I had been feeling returned along with life, but I was no longer the person I had been. I lay back in bed and began making plans about how to spend my life in service to humanity, giving rather than just trying to serve my own small wants and petty desires."

It was a vow she has kept for nearly forty years.

Audience with the Master

Today such encounters are called Near Death Experiences, or NDEs, but Wanda Sue calls it an audience with the Master.

She referred to the biblical phrase: In the beginning was the Word, and the Word was God…

Had she heard the voice of God? Or an interpreter from a higher spiritual plane who was capable of translating into language that she understood the first mystical lesson of her young life?

The true message imparted from a higher source on that fateful near-suicide night in 1959 was:

Rebirth is Law.

Wanda Sue had never heard about the theory of reincarnation; she nearly wished herself dead and in so doing found out that life is eternal.

"I didn't realize it then, but I'd just taken my first step onto the mystical path," she said, "and I am still taking my journey of a thousand miles on which motivation, not the act, is what counts."

According to Wanda Sue's understanding of suicide, it is not a hideous or heinous crime against the Creator. The only judgment to be made, if it can even be called judgment, is on the reason for taking one's own life, not the act that accomplishes the rendering of the body incapable of further sustaining the condition called life by men.

Justification for the Right to Die with Dignity

I think that in the case of my thirty-three-year-old son-in-law, his untimely, unavoidable death was just around the corner, so his choice may have been appropriate. But it is not for me to determine.

Could the same be said for a cancer victim begging to have the choice to die rather than prolong life through intense suffering? Possibly you have your own ideas about this subject. It has been in the news lately as various sides face each other in the battle for the right to life versus the right to choose death, one of the major political issues of the final decade of the twentieth century.

Choices and Decisions

We all may find ourselves faced with choices and decisions that fall into the moral and ethical arenas, choices and decisions that might not always bring favorable judgment from those who form opinions about such acts as we contemplate performing.

We must each be responsible for our own actions. We must each live with the choices and decisions we make. I recently chose to have a vasectomy because I decided that to bring one child into the world is enough, considering that there are too many people on the Earth now, and we are killing off the animals and other people and are polluting the water and the air.

I have a wonderful daughter. I have chosen to be the father of my one and only child. This raises the question: Do we have the right to carry out acts such as I carried out? In other words, is preventing life from manifesting a form of genocide?

Reverse Murder?

Can voluntary or enforced sterilization be construed as reverse murder? Unlike abortion, in which a baby's body is already forming before the possibility of its living on Earth is extinguished, is prevention of fetuses from even forming equal to preventing life from manifesting in the first place? Before making a judgment, consider the motivation for the act.

Case in Point

I knew a woman who had five children. Her husband had long since disappeared to evade the responsibility of raising his family.

One day I asked, "Have you ever considered the fact that there are too many people in the world? How will you ever feed your five children and yourself without a husband to help?"

Her answer was, "Jesus will take care of me."

How many people have starved to death while believing that Jesus would take care of them?

In the East, where death and life are considered to be a karmic wheel, both aspects of the One are interconnected. Karma is the Law of Cause and Effect. Under this great, immutable law, having too many children may have karmic implications as serious as denying life the right to manifest, or ending life after it has manifested.

Death, like birth, continues to remain one of the great mysteries that faces each of us.

The Lazarus Transition

A lady friend of mine named Frances works at a large hospital in Southern California on the graveyard shift. A year earlier, her father had died in the Philippine Islands and Frances had not been able to attend his funeral.

At three o'clock one morning, she was attending to a patient in his room. Frances sat down on a chair to rest because she was very tired.

Sometimes when a person is physically tired, the veil between the physical plane and the astral planes drops away. As Frances sat on the chair, she looked up and saw a man standing in the doorway. The man was her father. He was wearing a green sweater that she had bought for his birthday. They gazed at each other for what seemed to be about one minute. Then her father disappeared.

In the late 1980s, Frances was in the Philippines when her sister Elizabeth committed suicide. All of the family gathered together to attend the funeral, where they were able to view Elizabeth's body in the open casket. As they viewed the body, Frances's brother Frank became dizzy and lost consciousness. He fell to the floor. The voice of Elizabeth began to talk through Frank's mouth.

Elizabeth explained that she was sorry she had taken her own life, and said she wanted to get back into her body but it was destroyed by the poison she had taken. She said that her husband Raymond was an alcoholic and had physically abused her many times.

She said "Good luck" to everyone and ended her statements. Frank then regained consciousness.

Is it any wonder many mystics refer to death as "transition"—not a final ending, but a changing from one condition of existence to another?

Perhaps Lazarus truly did rise from the dead.

If so, maybe he is a symbol for all people who are born and eventually go through transition. In that respect, I am Lazarus…and so are you!

Final Thoughts

When people ask me what I do on the job, I say, "I'm the head man." That means I "clean the head," which is another term for rest room. I have worked in the field of janitorial services for much of my adult life. Another term for my job is "custodian." I like that because I love keeping things clean and orderly.

Many people think that janitorial work is humble. They think that the fact that I do that kind of work disqualifies me from writing a book about Jesus. In other words, I have no authority. In such situations I am reminded of the old saying: Don't judge a book by its cover. Jacob Boehme, a great humanitarian and mystic, was a shoemaker. And Jesus was a carpenter.

I realize this may sound egotistical, but consider the implication—not only in my life, but in all people's lives. Maybe I, or we, held power in the past, so much that the welfare of many others depended on our decisions. Or possibly in the future, a world leadership role awaits me—or you. Those occupied with peacekeeping on a mass scale rarely have time to investigate the mysteries and true meaning of life. Humble occupations have their definite advantages. Many of the benefits of my occupation in this lifetime are revealed in this book.

You might not agree with anything I've said; or maybe part of it will touch you, leaving you with questions.

I am a walking question mark.

Perhaps this book will help you become one, too.

Of all my experiences, I believe the most profound was my encounter with Jesus! Somehow I feel we'll meet again, on this Earth plane or the next. I hope you meet Him, too.

Along the way, enjoy your encounters—close or otherwise—within the many mansions of your own being. It all begins with that first step of the mythical "journey of a thousand miles" popularized by Rosicrucians and other philosophers throughout history.

May your days be filled with Life, Light, and Love as you journey along your own personal path to enlightenment.

Postscript

A commonly reported psychic phenomenon involves seeing someone who then disappears. It happens all over the world to everyday, down-to-earth, sane individuals—people like you and me.

When I was about thirty-three, I went to a local Los Angeles County health clinic for a blood test. The male nurse told me to sit in a chair directly in front of a refrigerator. He then put the needle in my left arm to draw blood and left the needle in the vein and walked away, telling me he would be right back.

But he became distracted by something else and forgot me. I do not enjoy the sight of blood and I became dizzy. I slipped in and out of the borderline state several times and I was sweating profusely. Each time I entered the borderline state I could see a nineteen-year-old girl sitting on top of the refrigerator directly behind me. She was wearing a long, loose, colorful dress. She was playing with my hair and asking me what I was doing in there .

About then, I was almost falling out of the chair when three nurses grabbed me and removed the needle. When I asked the three nurses who the young girl was, they looked at me in a strange way and said that no one in their right mind would be sitting on the refrigerator.

I think the young lady was either earthbound or just waiting for others to appear and guide her to the astral planes.

In a similar incident, a fellow janitor related to me how, when he lived near Mexico City, a strange thing happened to him and his friend.

About 2:00 A.M. they had left a party and were returning home on horseback. The moon was shining brightly and the horse they were riding was trotting slowly. They observed in the near distance a sixteen-year-old girl sitting on a wooden fence.

When the horse caught sight of the girl, it bolted in panic, running at full speed with both riders barely able to hold on.

As the horse raced along the path, the girl, wearing a long, flowing dress, was suddenly floating alongside the two startled riders, and her dress flapped loudly against their leather leg-coverings.

The rider in the rear pulled his pistol to shoot the girl, and my friend told him to put the gun away. Then the girl disappeared.

The same thing could happen to you.

If it does, welcome to the club!